14 KEYS TO
GREAT TRUTH PUZZLES

14 KEYS
TO
GREAT TRUTH
PUZZLES

JOHN LEE BAUGHMAN

DeVorss & Company
p.o. box 550
Marina del Rey, CA 90294–0550

ISBN: 0–87516–597–4
Library of Congress Card Catalog
Number: 87–072924

Printed in the United States of America

CONTENTS

PREFACE

I am sure that all of us agree life holds many secrets for us, otherwise we would live more serenely, more joyously and more abundantly. I suppose nearly everyone at one time or another has said to himself, "There must be an easier way to live." And there is! You know, there is a way of life, a teaching that actually holds the keys to life, that holds the secrets to life. This teaching is not just one great thing. It is *the* thing. It is that through which all other things are changed for the better. If we were to get a real good grasp of this teaching and seek to put it into practice, miracles would happen in our lives. What is this teaching? Well, it is simply putting God into our lives—not "buck up," "pull yourself together," "keep your chin up," "will yourself to the top," "look what Washington and Lincoln did." That is not the answer. That is not the teaching. The teaching that works is simply this—putting God into your life!

Through this kind of teaching we realize in our approach to life that our problem only has the size that we give it. The world says, "No, a problem has its own size." But not at all. Your grief, your frustration, your lack, your sickness has only the size you give it, only the evaluation you give it, only the estimate you give it.

You know *wickedness* as used in the Bible means leaving God, yes, that part of our lives where we have left out God. The word itself is derived from the Old English, meaning *be-witched* or *under a spell*; and in that sense, of course, all of us have a portion of this wickedness because all of us to a degree are under the spell of the world, its viewpoints, its values, its ways of gauging things. Frankly, there is not one of us that has not been to some degree deceived at one time or another into sickness, into some form of lack, into some form of frustration.

The great deception of the world, for example, in one instance is this: It tells us that sicknesses are things apart, each with its own germ, each with its own cause, and that they stand ready to attack us at random. You know, as though we had a body that we were just sort of dragging along with these things pouncing on it and infecting it. And of course, factually, this is true until we come into this teaching and through it learn certain great Truths that set us free, enabling us to nullify and render harmless these things that would attack us.

Another large portion of the great deception of the world is this: that fate and luck, as "inconstant as the moon" as Shakespeare poetically put it, sort of descend upon us all the time, hit us pellmell—and that, factually, is true. There is not one of us who hasn't said, "Just my luck," "Wouldn't that happen to me?" "When it rains it pours." Yes, but only until we get hold of this teaching and learn certain great Truths from it that set us free. Another portion of this great deception the world foists upon us is this: that outer things and people make us happy or unhappy. And factually you know with me that that has been true—but not necessarily so, when we come into this teaching and learn certain great Truths that set us free from all this.

Now proof that these factual experiences we have listed do not really represent life, and need not be a part of your future experiences, is found in this: As you begin to put God into your life, one by one these things dissolve into the nothingness from whence they have come. How do you put God into your life? By renewing your mind with spiritual ideas or that which you really belong to in God. If you exclude any side of your life—business, human relations or your body—from this practice you put it bigger than God.

The Bible in Psalm 51: verse 10 tells us, "Create in me a clean heart, O God." This means your heart, your subconscious mind, your feeling nature, that part of you where your convictions lie—a heart there where there is no further belief in negative things. Yes, all belief in sickness, all belief in poverty, all belief in obstacles, all belief in giving power to outer things and people, all belief in hatred and force and cunning, all belief in coveting that which belongs to somebody else, all belief in the past to destroy you. That is the requirement. One by one these things must be knocked out as they challenge us. You do this *not* by screwing up your will power and trying to force yourself past them like so many people have tried to do. Rather, you do it by the *Laughter of God*.

Now pray tell, what is the Laughter of God? Listen to this seriously for it is something deep and real and moving: It is a conviction in a per-

son, who is so convinced of God's presence and
that he belongs only to God, that nothing in him
any longer accepts his difficulty. Yes, I once gave
you a power and evaluation but now I give you
none. I give all power unto God and I am free
from you forever. God is my all in all. There is
no rival to God, and God's Lord or Law for me
is complete wholeness of body, supply sufficient
and to spare, an interesting and true place of
service always, and great joy. And my heart is
clean for that Higher Law to operate through me
by means of its Holy Spirit. So I now bear witness
to that Higher Law, God's Law of health, taking
charge of every department of my body and ordering it aright so that I now feel my body riding back, riding back on the healing Law of God.
Think about the promises, "I am the Lord that
healeth thee," "The Lord will perfect that which
concerneth thee," "I will restore health unto
you," "I will heal thee of thy wounds," "I will
take sickness out of the midst of thee." You cannot twist these promises. Think of them.

Also I bear witness to that Higher Law, the
Law of God's wealth, taking charge of my business affairs and ordering them aright so that I
now feel my business affairs riding back, riding

back to prosperity and wealth on the prospering Law of God. Think of this promise, "I am the Lord thy God which teacheth thee to profit, which leadeth thee by the way that thou shouldest go." Then, too, I bear witness to that Higher Law, the Law of God's harmony, taking charge of my human relations and ordering them aright so that I now feel my human relations riding back, riding back to happiness on the harmonizing Law of God. Think of this promise, "Peace I leave with you, my peace I give unto you: not as the world giveth, give I unto you."

Such is the Laughter of God. It is a conviction that dissolves the shadows of the great deception as readily as the mist before the morning sun. I see you in possession of that conviction now and laughing at your problem with the Laughter of God. How is He going to do it? None of your business. Your business from this preface is to learn to wait upon God, and with utter conviction know that He now goes before you and brings the answer to you!

I

INTUITION IS YOUR KEY TO ORIGINALITY— IT IS NOT ESP

Science has a way of getting a new name for whatever it has to offer, ever so many years. There is nothing wrong about that. It stirs up interest again.

For example, if today we were told that mental telepathy had an important part to play in our lives, people would say, "Well, that's old stuff. Much has been written about that." So we are given a new name for it—ESP or Extra Sensory Perception—and everybody gets excited. People begin to study it again as though it were something new.

Now I am not intending here to demean ESP. I have spent some years in researching the psychic side of life, and mental telepathy is one of the more simple forms of it. Boiled down, it suggests that you and I can make another person think of us, and that we can also contact the thoughts of another person through developing mental

1

telepathy. These are both plausible and a part of life.

But at no time does mental telepathy or ESP reach *beyond* the human level. It has been given many overtones in current writings, which equate it with parapsychology and other such things. But it still deals with just the human level.

Here I want to take you into *deeper waters*. Into something that is many light-years in advance of ESP. And you are the kind that can grasp this and use it in your life. For you have always sought to go to the highest Source for everything, and we are about to do that now.

Our subject is, "Intuition, Man's Greatest Faculty"—with no apologies whatsoever for that claim. I should like to introduce it to you in a rather novel way. In studying and reading the scriptures, also in studying and reading metaphysics, we constantly hear of dimensions. But I am not sure that everyone is clear as to what they are. Whether we are or not, we can stand to refresh our minds a bit on the subject of dimensions as a kind of preface to intuition.

What is a dimension? A dimension is simply a direction. That is all. The first dimension is forward and back. The second dimension is across, which is quite different from forward and back. The third dimension is up and down, which is still different from the other two.

Now there is still another dimension which we cannot picture as yet. Though we can talk about it. Yes, we can concede a fourth dimension, to which we are often referred, but we could not imagine it in detail. Why? Human beings are, in particular, three-dimensional beings. That is, they understand what it is to go forward and back. They understand what it is to go across. And they understand what it is to go up and down. But that is all!

What would a one-dimensional creature be? Well, it would be one that could imagine going only forward and back on a straight line. It might go in all directions, but it thinks it is a straight line. For example, it might go across or up and down, but it would not know the difference. To it, there is just one dimension. It senses only going forward and back on a straight line.

A snail, for illustration, cannot imagine going sideways or up and down. You may see it move sideways or climb up a wall. But it does not know it. It just has a sense of moving forward and back on a straight line. Do not feel sorry for it, though. It is not even aware of its limitations. That is its world.

A second-dimensional creature is quite different. It can sense two dimensions. It knows what it is to go not only forward and back, but also across. You cannot fool it with just one dimension. As soon as it reaches a wall, it too may climb up that wall. But again it does not know, in this instance, that it is going up and down. It just knows forward and back. Then across.

However, a human being is still different from that. He is three-dimensional. He knows what it is to go forward and back as well as across. But he also knows what it is to go up and down. He is aware of all dimensions on this plane.

Now again, as human beings, though we can hear about and read about a fourth dimension to come—we cannot imagine it. We are strictly three-dimensional beings up 'til now. I want to stress the fact, though, that *heaven is not the fourth dimension*. Some writers get carried away with that fourth dimension and try to make it into heaven. But heaven is on all planes—and so is hell!

So you and I can walk forward and back, go across, move up and down. But that is all for now. We are three-dimensional beings. Some day we will be fourth-dimensional beings, and then it will be perfectly natural for us. I want to say, at this juncture, that you are on the way to expressing heaven, which is deep within you. Everyone who comes into this study is definitely going to express more and more of heaven. I know that you are glad to hear that—whatever may be the hell through which you are presently passing.

When I say that you are going to express more and more of heaven, that does not mean you are going to die right away. You do not have to die to get into heaven. You have to live a little more. Apropos of that, I might add, do not try to stay on this plane too long. Do not try to shuffle off too soon. Do not worry about the next plane—the fourth dimension. Do not be too concerned about the last plane on which you were. Just get the most out of this one. That is a vital part of living.

When you do go to the next plane or the next world—some of you may doubt that, but whether you doubt it or not you are still going. So I just thought I would mention it—yes, when you do go to the next plane or the next world, it will be fourth-dimensional. As a matter of fact, I might add here that one thousand years from now you will still be somewhere—alive and kicking. Under your breath you may be saying, "I hope not. Don't tell me there is more of this to endure." But whether you think so or not—it will happen!

So when you go to the next plane or the next world it will be fourth-dimensional, and it may take a while before you get used to it. But that is not so unusual. After all, this plane puzzled you a bit when you first came.

You have forgotten it now. But in learning to eat your baby food you first got it into your ear more than your mouth for quite a spell. You needed to learn coordination. That was all. So it may be a while before you get used to the fourth dimension when you first enter into it. However, you will finally become accustomed, and then it will be perfectly natural for you.

But for now, the instrument of the three-dimensional world is the intellect. You are very conversant with that. It is standard equipment for everyone, you know, and it is that by which most people live their lives. But, thank goodness, we have a higher faculty than the intellect by which to run our lives, when we awaken to it. However, the intellect and the awakening to this higher faculty are *both* most important. As a matter of fact, some people could do with a little more intellect.

Some pious, well-meaning people talk an awful lot of rubbish. Some of them say, because they think they are very advanced, "I don't believe in the intellect." Have you ever heard that? Well, I believe them. They act the part. They could do with more intellect!

We have an infinitely more important faculty, however, and it is for that reason that I share this information. It is *intuition*! It is not limited to the usual description you hear about it on this plane. It is a very deep subject—not a surface one. When a person is open to intuition, responsive to it, it means teaching from the inside. That means contact with God individualized within you—a living contact with Him. The greatest asset you and I own is our divine faculty of intuition, when we become fully awakened to it.

Tuition is something else again. Most people, if you were to ask them to define it, would say, "Oh that is how much you pay when you go to college." But that is not the real meaning of tuition. The real meaning is this: teaching from the outside. Tuition or teaching from the outside can let you down now and then. But never intuition, once you get onto it. Why? Because this teaching from within is *the pure Spirit of God*. So when you have that working for you, you cannot go wrong.

However, you must be sure that it is intuition, and not just your own feeling—on some matter at hand. You know, sometimes people have a strong feeling about something, and right away they call it intuition. But it may not be intuition at all. That is why I seek to help you over this hurdle.

This is where the intellect comes in handy. To find out whether the feeling by which you are being prompted is intuition or not—*your intellect can check for you.* If the feeling you have about something is silly, it is not intuition. If the feeling you have just wants your own way above the good of all others concerned, again it is not intuition. If a sense of hurry or excitement accompanies your feeling, it is not intuition. Intuition comes to you calmly, gloriously. But it does not bring with it excitement. Again, if there is any sense of rush connected with the feeling you have, then it is only the psychic realm you are experiencing. This hunch is not intuitive.

Does it matter what may be the source of your feeling? Does it matter whether it comes—from the psychic realm—or from intuition? Well, it is imperative that you be able to determine whence it has come. And this is why: Psychic feeling sometimes is right, depending upon where it got its information. But intuition, when it comes to you, is always right. Why? Because it is the very Spirit of God Himself directing you!

Remember always, intuition being completely the action of Spirit—God's Holy Spirit—can never err. Can never make a mistake. So when you have it for your guidance you cannot go wrong in your decision. And intuition, quite apart from the psychic realm, comes to you differently. It comes to you serenely, friendly, calmly, gently—like the dawn of a new day.

Now why is it important to develop your intuition? What are its practical relations to your affairs? Well, it is the very Spirit of God seeking to inspirit itself in you—inspire you where you need it—guide you where you need it. It is that important! So it comes to you as inspiration for your life. And again, while it has no form of itself, being Spirit, it will come into form according to the shape of your mind. There is where it takes shape, like water seeking the shape of its banks. This is why natural lakes are so much more beautiful than artificial ones. Just as water seeks its natural banks, so does inspiration, the Spirit of God, intuition, seek the shape of your mind.

For example, when intuition comes to a musician, it comes as music. When intuition comes to an engineer, it comes to him in the machinery with which he deals. When intuition comes to a painter, it comes as visions of pictures. When intuition comes to a writer, it comes to him as stories that have never been written. When intuition comes to a businessman, it comes to him pertinent to his business deals. It is as realistic as that.

What I have described is wholly the activity of intuition. And it comes to all of us at times as warnings—believe it or not. Yes, whenever you are in danger—something in your body, for example, that has not come to the surface. Something in your human relations. Something in your business. It would seek to warn you of that danger, so that you can do something about it now before it fully happens in the outer.

If you have not received such a warning in your life, it does not disprove the existence of intuition. It merely indicates the reason could be that there has been too much static in your consciousness. Or you have been too opinionated. Or you have been too undeveloped spiritually. Or there has been too much of a sense of importance on your part.

Sometimes intuition comes as a vague kind of fear, not a warning—just a vague kind of fear. And that fear seemingly is unattached to anything you know of, yet you have this fear. The way to clear that up—once you are onto the fact that intuition can come to you as such—is to go back to the Spirit of God and ask that it be made clear where you need guidance. And you will be shown!

Now when you develop your response sufficiently to intuition, it frequently comes as promptings of advice. Better advice than any human being—with the best use of ESP—could give you. Better advice than parapsychology associated with ESP—a person seemingly guiding you from another plane—could give you. Yes, when you develop your response sufficiently to intuition, it frequently comes as promptings of advice—the best you will ever get. Here is something that lives with you: If two courses are open in your life, one not nearly as good as the other, but you do not know it, and you need the correct prompting—intuition will make you to know which is the better road to take.

Then, too, all original ideas are given us by our intuition. If you have not had an original idea in your lifetime as yet, it shows your brain has been unused that way as far as this particular faculty is concerned. At least I have one original idea to my credit. That is the book I have written called, *Beyond Positive Thinking*—its subtitle: *The Greatest Secret Ever Told*. Nobody to my knowledge in all the writings of metaphysics ever quite hit upon that secret, which is the hub of that book!

Many metaphysicians know techniques of demonstrations that work. For instance, I think of one: A person was ill. Paralyzed in one half of his body. He was asked, "What would you do if you were well again—in good shape?" "Oh," he said, "I would go mountain climbing in the morning. Then play golf in the afternoon. Then a little tennis in the evening." He was told, "Imagine that you are doing these things already." Through such imaginings, he got his healing.

But do you know what that surface technique was based upon? The same thing that is in my book but put in deeper language, "See what the Father is doing," and "Go and do likewise." Now that is an original idea. It did not originate with me. Nor do any original ideas originate in a person. They originate in God. But if you are sufficiently interested in intuition, original ideas will begin to come to you from God.

Now if you develop your *imagination* positively, that also is important. It will help you *improve* upon your ideas, but the ideas will *not* be *original*. Imagination *improves*, but does not *originate*. However, *intuition* will give you *originality*. All metaphysicians and psychologists would agree that the rarest quality in the individual is originality, that it has occurred much less often than any other thing.

Well now, since originality comes from intuition, through cultivating it, you can get an original idea even though you have never had one up to now. The idea may not be of any great magnitude. You see, it will come according to the magnitude of your consciousness—that for which you are ready, *the next step* in the new things God has for you; *not more* than that for which you are ready, but the next good thing for you. So you may be sure one of my favorite Bible passages is, "Behold I would do a new thing through you; now it shall spring forth; shall ye not know it?" That is a favorite of mine because I seek always to do the new thing I have never done as yet.

Here is another application of how intuition will work for you. If there is a certain kind of information or data you need, and you must lay hold of such to complete a thesis or something you are writing—well, intuition will bring that data to you.

I think of the true story of a man who was writing such a work. It had to do with something long in the past. Seemingly he could not lay hold of certain information he needed on that subject. It seems that the writings on that subject were sort of obsolete—out of print.

Yet he had to have this information to complete his work. So he prayed about it. Opened himself intuitively to God. And one day he found himself in this city at an open bookstall, featuring old books. Most people cannot go by such a place, if it is outside, without thumbing through a few books. A book seemed to loom up right in front of him, and it had to do with this information he wanted. Now how in the world could that happen save through God?

Again, if there is a certain step that you should or should not take in business or whatever—to sign a lease or not to sign a lease, to go into partnership or not to go into partnership—well, if you will listen gently to your intuition, you will be made to know the thing to do. That is worth quite a bit right there.

Now that I have titillated your desire for this faculty a little, how are you going to develop intuition? THE FIRST STEP in developing intuition is to know that you have it as much as anyone who has ever lived. It is an existing faculty in you. It is not something reserved for women, as you have heard over the years. Perhaps the reason for that old-wives' tale is that women tend to operate more from their feeling natures. But it does nothing to change the fact that intuition is within every one of us equally. Yes, even though the consciousness of most people has largely been asleep to this greatest of all faculties—everyone has intuition.

Here is the *follow-through* of that first step: Think about intuition frequently—along the lines we have seen. Do it two or three times a week for awhile. Remind yourself that you have intuition, and that God is developing it in you. This is THE SECOND STEP.

There is one thing about these steps. There is nothing vague. You will know exactly what I said by the time I get through.

Now, then, for THE THIRD STEP in developing intuition: Begin building in greater peace of mind than you have had. That means freeing yourself from any resentments you may have. Getting rid of criticism. And dropping this business of self-importance. You know, in building a house you have to smooth off the ground. This may be necessary before intuition comes alive for you. So getting this greater peace of mind is the third step.

THE FOURTH STEP for developing intuition is this: When you come to intuition, remember you can no longer give orders. You cannot train it. You cannot manage it. It is bigger than any human being. When it comes to intuition, you can only listen. In other words, you must become the pupil of intuition. Are you willing?

With intuition there is always a sense of the presence of God in your thought. But you do not hear a voice. You would not know whether God had a French or Spanish accent. If you hear a voice—whatever the accent—you did not hear God. There you are only dealing with the psychic realm again.

With God, you will feel an inner prompting.

That is how God talks to you through intuition. It is the "still, small voice" of the Bible. You feel the direction in which you are to go. It will teach you things that no outer teacher ever could. About your human relations. About your finances. About your body. And so forth.

Finally, consider THE FIFTH STEP in developing intuition. This step is so important! Think of your body, your human relations, your home, your business—as expressions of Spirit, not as separate things. This is one of the greatest arts you can learn. Yes, train yourself to think of your body, your human relations, your finances, and so forth, as expressions of Spirit—not as separate things. Then, when you want intuition along a certain line, you will have already properly conditioned yourself to think of that thing as an expression of Spirit. And intuition will come to you—to show you the way as no man can!

Then, every day, through these five steps, intuition will be developing in you. Preventing you from mistakes that you would otherwise make. And giving you something different from anyone else—unique and original ideas.

Yes, if you will practice opening your intuition, you will find that while for the present you are still a three-dimensional being—you are no longer limited to a three-dimensional world. A new world will begin to open for you, a world that your "eyes and ears have not seen nor heard" as yet. Why? Because intuition will help you develop, in turn, those conditions of consciousness that you need for more abundant living than you have ever known!

II

IMAGINATION IS YOUR KEY TO IMPROVEMENT

Here we are dealing with imagination, but I want to share these THREE PREFACES first with you. They are rather startling. Make you think. However, we will need this *background* before *receiving the prefaces*. The following background carries weight quite apart from anything that I may do to embellish it.

You know, a great many people have some knowledge of hypnotism. I endorse it only in its clinical use in hospitals in certain cases of childbirth, where the mother cannot use an anesthetic, and so forth; and in dentistry, where it is used clinically in similar cases of negative reaction to anesthesia. It is no panacea, but it has its place in the scheme of things. Under experiments of hypnosis, what follows about the imagination was brought out. And it is very helpful.

We are concerned here about hypnosis in which a person is hypnotized by an outside agent—not self-hypnosis. A certain person was put into a coma; that is, his conscious mind went into a coma. His subconscious then believed everything that the hypnotist gave to it, because his conscious mind was in that coma. When the hypnotist told him that he was at the North Pole, he shivered. When told that his finger was on a hot stove, he reacted violently as though it were burned. It was done, too, with a weight-lifter, and he lifted more weight. Also a prizefighter, and he fought better.

This is the interesting thing about these last two experiments: Neither the weight-lifter nor the fighter had any more ability through the hypnotic spell. But conflicts, which each had, were relieved from their conscious minds. For example, the weight-lifter thought he could lift just so much. That is, his conscious mind thought so; but it was blotted out temporarily, and he did better. Now the fighter had a certain amount of disbelief about his ability, no matter how much he bragged about it consciously. However, his conscious mind being in a coma temporarily, he too did better.

What is the purpose of my telling you this?

Well, first, it proves that your subconscious does not know of itself the *difference between factual things and imagination*. And this is my FIRST prefacing point before undertaking the study of the imagination.

Let us put it another way—and this is my SECOND prefacing point: A human being always acts, feels and performs in accordance with what he *imagines* to be true about himself and his environment. Yes, whether it is factual or not, the human being acts, feels and performs in accordance with what he imagines to be true about himself and his environment. So what we are getting to again is that *you act and feel not necessarily according to how things really are in your life, but according to the image your mind has about it*. If you think that through, you will agree.

Now one other prefacing point—and this is my THIRD and final one: *If your imagination then is vivid enough, and detailed enough about anything you wish to demonstrate, your subconscious will now carry out what God has already prepared for you*—for a certainty. Is this helpful to you? Here you have had, not the subject proper, but THREE PREFACES to what I want to share with you.

With these as a kind of preparation, let us see what we can do. Basically, we are going to consider the quickest way to change your consciousness for the better, and that is to build in the faculties that you need. Make them usable. First we built in intuition, as man's greatest faculty. And I am sure that was an eye-opener, because it is leagues ahead of anything people would be likely to think—leagues ahead of ESP or Extra Sensory Perception, for example.

Now we are going to build in *imagination*, which is a kind of *twin to intuition* in that it works hand in glove with intuition, which I will prove in the body of this subject. And I call the two of them the "Gold Dust Twins" in their ability to produce.

I want to make this distinction in particular about these two. Intuition is totally a divine faculty and cannot be used in any other way. Thus, if you are prompted from a feeling within to do something, and it turns out to be a mistake, you have to know that it was not intuition. Because intuition, properly understood, is the *pure activity of the Spirit of God, and cannot err*.

On the other hand, imagination is something else. It is a human as well as a divine faculty. Therefore, it can be used both ways—positively and negatively. If your imagination is negative but highly developed, it will actually be successful in bringing carloads of trouble to you.

Let me cite several examples of how people use their imagination negatively—and think nothing of it. Recognize these phrases? I am not making them up. They are from life: "Just my luck." How long has it been since you heard that one? "Not the man I used to be. The years are bound to tell, you know." Heard that one lately? "Strain will show every time, sooner or later." Know that one? All right. Such people are just making what they are talking about more vivid for themselves. At the same time they are boring others to death. Not to mention their exaggerated imaginings about their operations, you know. Other people would walk a mile in their bare feet to hear about that! But they still tell them.

Yet imagination is so important, a book could be written about it. While intuition is unique in that it gives you original ideas, imagination, if used properly, improves everything in your life. Notice the difference. Intuition is unique in its ability to give you original ideas. But imagination, if used properly, improves everything in your world. It literally builds your world, if you begin to use it positively.

Now what is imagination? It is your image-making faculty, sometimes called the "scissors" of the mind. Its capacity is to make new images for your life. Better images than you are now actually enjoying. And whatever you begin to imagine with *feeling*, you build into your world!

The Bible tells us much about the breaking up of images. But that is not a reference to the images in your imagination. Those were the ancient idols they had then. If, though, you have been carrying around negative pictures in your mind all you life, you need to start calling them *causes* for all the negative *effects* in your world—and get rid of them. For you are worshipping negative images in your imagination.

Let us get away here from ourselves for a moment to lift the burden. I knew an engineer once—should have been more intelligent—who collected books, medical books on human ailments, with harrowing pictures. What do you think it did for him? He imagined all kinds of negative things about himself. He did not have to wait for the medical profession to dig up some new disease and name it; he could anticipate getting it. He dreamed up things all by himself from these pictures. Then, too, some people do not stop with imagining negative things about their bodies. They do it for others for free.

Always imagine the best about your body— always strong, always healthy. Never mind if you are sick at the moment. This is the way to get well.

So you build imagination into your consciousness. How? This positive way: You build it into your consciousness by thinking about it. And get this! If you begin positively imagining new images for your body, your subconscious will not know whether they are *factual* or just *imagined*. It will simply begin to take you that way. So, to build imagination in, begin to think about it, what it can do for you. Train yourself to imagine things you want to come into your human relations, and ask God to give you more such imaginings. That is the way to build it into your consciousness.

Let us turn to your business for a moment, with a practical application. Start imagining things you have never seen as yet in your business. Certain activities that you would like to have as a part of your business—but *are not* as yet. Imagine them anyway! Begin doing this: Attach your imagination to something in your business. Imagine that part of your business improved, and have faith in God to bring it about. Now that is an exact application. Try it! *Remember again*, your subconscious does not know the difference between what you are imagining and the facts of the case. So it will start to let your newly imagined results begin to come.

Thus, if you want to build a success in life, you will have to have imagination, your image-making faculty, *going for you*. So practice it, now that you understand why it will work. Many people have their imagination highly developed in a positive manner. Composers, writers,

painters have to do it. Shakespeare and Balzac,
for example, invented characters but borrowed
plots. Different with Dickens, though—he invented plots but his characters actually existed.
They dress differently today, but if you have read
Dickens lately, reviewed it, such characters are
going about right now in any great city. That is
what makes it all so interesting.

This was true of Edison, too. He had a strong
imagination. Most people forget that he was
called the "practical inventor." Most people just
think of him as a great inventor. But he was always thinking of something that "paid off," if you
will remember. So they called him the "practical
inventor." He was asked why that tag was given
to him, and his answer was that he always looked
around to see what was needed. Yes, what the
people did not have and would use, if someone
could dream it up. Then he began to imagine
how that could be worked out. Finally his *intuition* gave him the answer. Why? Because *intuition* works through the *imagination*, when
imagination cooperates—just as he was doing.
Sort of imagining how a side of life could be better. Thus *intuition* was *"milked"* to give the *ideas*
of how to do it.

In Edison's time, for example, to prove my point, they had the arc lamp but it was cumbersome. The mechanism was much too large to put into a home. So Edison imagined heating a filament and putting it into a vacuum, you will remember. Tried about a thousand experiments, but finally made it. Now most people do not do that. They think the way to do something is the way it has been done—and that is all there is to it.

You know, prior to the time the typewriter came around, people had been using steel pens. Before that, they had quills. Do any of you remember the quill? If you had a good duck feather or goose feather and shaped one end of it like a pen point to make it write, you had a quill. When steel pens took the place of quills, it was interesting. People said, "If God wanted steel pens He would have made them that way instead of quills." You have heard that refrain, have you not? It has been around a long time—with anything new. But finally the typewriter superseded steel pens, which up 'til then had been used in business exclusively. However, the typewriter was not a great success, either, right off. For quite a while, believe it or not, typewritten copies were not allowed in the courtrooms. Did you know that? Gives you some idea of how slow the process of expansion in life really is—and why!

Now everybody has intuition and imagination——these "Gold Dust Twins." It is a matter of putting them to work. You see, they have been lying there dormant to some degree. Here is direct use: if an idea comes to you first, direct from your intuition—think it out, formulate it, act on it. That is the imagination in follow-through action. Now let us see how you can further prime the pump of intuition with your imagination:

Whatever I have said up 'til now, you do not think it is so because I said it. But because something within you intuitively tells you, "That is true for my body, it could be healed," "That is true about my next place of service, it could happen," "That is true about any mess in my human relations, it could be straightened out." Intuitively, then, you know all this is true. That is why you agree.

Instead of just agreeing, which is very decent of you, begin to understand what your *intuition* has told you—that these are right ideas about you. So begin to *imagine* them. Use your imagination with that right idea about your body. Act on it. Imagine that part of your body healed. Imagine yourself in that job. Do it in your meditation times. Imagine the beautiful working out in your human relations also, remembering that the subconscious does not know the difference between factuality and imagination. Yes, as soon as you *live with a new image*, your subconscious will begin to move you toward it.

This intuitive and imaginative approach does not have to begin and end with the three ways in which I used it in meditation periods for your body, your human relations and your business. It could be a new idea of how to dress, if you are tired of the way in which you groom. It could be a new idea of how to redecorate your home, if you are tired of the way your home looks. It could be a new idea of how to run your life, if there has been too much disorder in it.

Some people have plenty of imagination, but they use it all negatively. It is interesting to note here what the same practice *reversed* could do. For example, take someone with a highly developed imagination, but all negative. He imagines people are talking about him. He imagines that people are working against him. He imagines the craziest things are taking place in his body. Give him the slightest negative suggestion about anything, and he will go for it wholeheartedly. Now that is a highly developed negative imagination. *Turn it around*, and this person could do great things in his life. He already has his imagination developed—but in the wrong direction.

You see, the thief imagines or fancies himself to be a thief. The liar imagines or fancies himself to be quite a liar. The curse here is that he cannot believe anyone else. The sick person imagines himself sick. It hurts a person to hear that. He says, "This is not imagination, I've got it." Yes, but that is how he got it! Not intentionally, of course. However, he either imagined a negative suggestion, owned a general fear, or nourished a bad disposition—to get it!

To continue. A poor person imagines pictures of poverty, frustration and futility about his person. He may never speak of it, but he cannot hide the results. Now I am not saying that in condemnation. I am saying let us have done with it. Let us open ourselves to the opulent life God wants for us. Let us begin to live!

You see, everyone presents to the world his own idea of himself. This is interesting. What idea do you have of yourself? What idea, in particular, do you have of your human relations? What idea do you have of your supply—honestly now? You do not like it—once you have faced it? Well, thank God, you can change it. That is your prerogative. Emerson said what I have just described: that "Man surrounds himself with his own image." But once he faces that, any part of it he does not like—he can change!

You see, the Truth student is about the practice of presenting God's image and likeness of the Son there. God's image and likeness for his human relations. God's image and likeness for that part of his body—its perfect function. "Wist ye not that I must be about my Father's business?" the Bible tells us.

What would you like other people to think of you? Well, be the thing in your imagination that you want to be—that new image. Then your subconscious has to start carrying it out, moving forward with it. *Remember again*, your subconscious does not know the difference between *factuality* and *imagination*.

Let us take something specific. Say you want to be a musician. Now I am not saying you do. But if you do, think it over. Pick out some instrument and imagine yourself playing it well, and doing it as a job. If you want to write—amazing how many people want to, and have never written—well, you will need more than paper and pencil. Imagine what you should write about. Open up your intuition to give you an idea, the idea you need. Then, as you begin your writing, right there at the outset imagine the publisher who will publish your writings. So many writers, you know, leave that out. Then, after they get the book written, they wonder why they do not have a publisher. All of which is part of the same program.

In closing I want to say this: For heaven's sake, stop thinking of a new idea as some kind of a personal affront. Such as, "Oh, my heavens, do I have to have a new idea? I never had a new idea in my whole life!" Yes, stop thinking of it as a personal affront. It belongs to you. It can happen to you. Stop being in the way. Your mind is an open end for God here. So open up your intuition. You have the right to all kinds of good ideas. As the saying goes, "From the neck up you are worth quite a fortune, but from the neck down only a few cents."

As you open yourself to new ideas for your life, do it in conjunction with the positive use of your imagination. Because the positive use of your imagination is terrific mental and spiritual training. And it is fun!

How again do you build in imagination? You build in imagination by thinking about it. Let us go back to this premise: I am going to start using my imagination, and I am going to imagine that gland of mine, that organ, as functioning perfectly. I am going to imagine this also in general about my body: that it is changing for the better. Why? Because I now understand that my subconscious does not know the difference between imagination and factuality. If I begin to present this new image, live with it, then that is the way my body will go. By like token, if I begin to imagine some very real changes for the better in my business, the subconscious again does not know the difference between factuality and imagination—and my business must begin to go that way. The same must necessarily also take place in my human relations, as I begin to imagine them in the most favorable light.

Thus, you are going to begin imagining all the things you would like to come into your life. Because your subconscious does not know the difference between factuality and imagination, you are going to imagine them as being done NOW in your life. Imagine them in detail. *And the more vivid, the more detailed, the sooner they will happen.* As you do this, ask God to give you more such imaginings. To make you a whole new being through the use of your imagination. To improve everything in your world.

Remember this as a finality. Whatever you imagine with FEELING, you build into your world!

III

GOD'S MOTHERING SPIRIT CAN BRING
BACK THOSE—WHO WORSHIP GOD
ONLY AS IMPERSONAL LAWS—TO THE
PERSONAL CARING OF GOD

When the discovery was made that *God operated by law* and not whimsy—man took a great step forward in understanding. It meant that God was impartial, unprejudiced and without favoritism in bestowing His blessing of "life more abundant." That is, if you worked lovingly and correctly with His laws of health, harmony and prosperity, you would receive an abundance of these blessings with *certainty*.

Why? Because *Holy Spirit*, the means by which God acts through man, would move upon you *as the loving Power behind His laws* and bring them to pass.

Unfortunately some students of metaphysics, having made the discovery that *God operates by law*, then began to think their God was *nothing more than a set of impersonal laws*. Here they merely lost their perspective. *The laws* are simply *the loving ways* in which God works. God is still God, you see. These laws are simply His ways of operating.

What is God, then? Well, what are you? You are a composite of qualities—life, love, wisdom, power and substance—individualized into the presence that you are. Through them you know that you are alive. Well, God is like that, too. He is a composite of the same qualities *but in their full blossom*. Thus He is able to share *more* of each of these qualities with you as you are ready. *Another helpful* point to grasp here is that though you are of *the same nature in qualities* as God, He is *everywhere equally present* while you are His potential expression only in *the spot* you occupy.

Then, too, even as you *know yourself to be alive* because of these qualities, even so, you must also know that God is alive *for the same reason*. After all, He created you out of His own qualities; and *if you are alive, how much more so is He!* This is why He is able to hold out to you a "life more abundant" than you have ever known.

All of which brings us to the mothering Spirit of God, the means by which He cares for us and works through us. Holy Spirit is that influencing phase of God that causes us to aspire to having the *Higher Laws of God manifested in our lives.* And it is why the Bible tells us in John 4:23, "But the hour cometh, and now is, when the true worshippers shall worship the Father in Spirit and in Turth: for the Father seeketh such to worship Him."

When we finally come to worship God as Spirit, we will know Him *to be like a good mother in her love for her child*—but with an *ability* that is NOT finite as a mother's; rather, INFINITE to help us.

Yes, when Spirit moves in, sickness moves out. When Spirit moves in, poverty moves out. When Spirit moves in, inharmony and loneliness move out. Why? Because Holy Spirit is the mothering Spirit by which God personally cares and the right arm by which He acts through us. Our authority for this is Ezekiel 37:14. "And I shall put my Spirit in you, and ye shall live." That is what God is saying all though the Bible—that He will put His Spirit in us, and we shall live! Think what that means. It means your life will be joyous, active and progressive—not just an existence.

To receive His Spirit regularly as the inspiration of our lives, we need to know that our part is to realize that Holy Spirit is not just a vague something to be used only to conjure up great visions like the prophets of old—as some people imagine. Rather, it is the influencing phase of God that is with us always to sustain us, heal us, prosper us, make contacts for us, establish harmony in our lives and guide us. In other words, the essential point to remember is that it is always there to be used for all everyday practical purposes.

Yes, if we have papers to sign, it will reveal to us whether or not we should. If we have a business step to take, it will guide us. If we are thinking of going into partnership, it will warn us against it or move us to do so. If it is a healing you need, a healing it will produce for you. If it is prosperity you need, supply it will stir up for you. If it is contacts you need, contacts it will make for you in the strangest of ways. If it is order you need, it will take charge of your affairs and establish just that!

And that brings to mind that grand old axiomatic statement of metaphysics, "*There is always a price or penalty in life.*" In this instance, the price is spiritual treatment on a regular basis— or the penalty of no demonstration.

So without further ado, let us *learn how to treat* and *pay the price of treatment*—that we may have Holy Spirit in our lives as an active agent to fulfill our every need. The price of successful cooperating with Holy Spirit is furnishing it with the *proper conditions* in our consciousness for its entrance in and through us.

The *first* condition to set up is peace of mind. To accomplish this—stop thinking about your problem and start thinking on God. *Then* you must believe that God can positively do anything. Many churchgoers would be shocked to hear that. Why? Because in their secret hearts they are not too sure. That is why they constantly ask the minister, "But do you know of a case like mine being handled?"

Finally, you must *lay hold of the right concept* and *charge it up with feeling*. Holy Spirit will take care of the rest. That *feeling of yours*, you see, will eventually be *the very Spirit of God*, overwhelming your subconscious and taking charge of your case. *This is literally feeling your way to the heights*!

Remember, always, regardless of your situation, you have but one problem—and that is to *lay hold of the right concept* and then *get that right concept into your subconscious* or *feeling nature*. How do you lay hold of that right concept? Well, you are dealing with *Holy Spirit* here. So the simplest way would be to use it as the basis of your concept. For example, "The very Holy Spirit of God is (healing me now) or (prospering me) or (taking me to my true place of employment) or (establishing order and companionship in my life) or (making me to know the right decision)."

How do you charge up that right concept with feeling? Through *suggestive reiteration of that right concept in your conscious mind*. This suggestive reiteration will put that right concept down into your subconscious with ease and gentleness. Much like a crane lifts a huge crate and puts it down into the hold of a ship.

Considering the fact that *Holy Spirit works at full pressure through the individual when It has this kind of cooperation from him*—you simply owe it to yourself to set up definite spiritual treatment periods throughout the week.

To get steady, reliable help from your God, there needs to be at least *one treatment period every twenty-four hours, preferably two. And in an emergency, three*, until the emergency has passed. A ten- or fifteen-minute period is long enough. Time is not the important thing here— *realization is*: how much you *feel God doing that wonderful thing through you*. And it is helpful *to forget the treatment and the thing for which you are treating*—until you return to treatment again. Why? It lets Holy Spirit continue its work in all the *unconscious moments* between treatments.

This is how to experience the mothering Spirit of God—to have a God that really cares!

IV

PRECISELY (NO GENERALITIES PLEASE) WHAT IS SUBSTANCE?

The term *substance* is the most *misued* in the study of Truth—for one simple reason: it is the least *understood*! I purposely once asked a group of six outstanding Truth students—to define substance for me *as the term is used in metaphysics*. I got six different answers—all general. With due respect, generalities won't do here. Students have the tendency to define substance in terms of *many different qualities* of God. But substance is ONLY ONE facet of God. And its place and its function need to be known *exactly*.

Unless one has a precise knowledge of *each* aspect of God—in this instance SUBSTANCE— then the total sides to His Presence in one's life *lack the cohesion* that make for demonstration.

The *dictionary* defines substance as "that which underlies *all* outward manifestation"— meaning, then, that which stands under *both* good and bad. But *metaphysics* defines "the substance of God as the realm of divine ideas in Divine Mind." Therefore the word "substance" has a *different* meaning in metaphysics than the world's definition.

That is the reason we often say in the study of Truth that sickness, misery and poverty have *no* substance in them. Because not one of these is substantiated by God. They are substantiated ONLY by *beliefs* from *ideas* of the race that get into you. That is all. You could not have any one of these challenges without such belief.

Now here we are going to set about displacing any such belief from the world that may have found acceptance in you—with a great Truth. *That of an idea of perfection or substance from this realm of divine ideas.* And let it actually gain entrance into your subconscious—until it substantiates that part of your life in need.

To do so, let us clearly understand this basic point: The *only substance* that exists in Divine Mind is an idea of perfection for anything in your life. And it will substantiate that thing "all the way into its form or manifestation"—if you let it—because the substance idea, being an idea, *cannot be seen of itself.* Yet it is that which stands under—or substantiates all the way—what *it wants to come into form or manifestation*!

This is the way it works! When you spiritually treat or correctly pray for a certain part of your life, Holy Spirit, the means by which God acts through man, *moves its substance idea forward in you*—into your subconscious—replacing your old belief from the negative race idea—and then up into your body or human relations or financial world. (*Obviously, then, it is not something limited to prosperity.*)

Now that you have seen how it works, let me say that *correct placement of faith* on your part affords the *greatest entrance* known for *substance* to enter this plane to your affairs. That is why it says in the Bible, "*Faith* is the *substance* of *things hoped for*, the *evidence* of things *not seen.*"

So it must be said, that while the IDEAS that could save our lives have their origin in Divine Mind, man has put the limitations of his negative thinking upon the very things he wants to have happen. *This must stop*! We are going to be precise. We are going to let our needed good happen through this "get together" in spiritual reasoning and faith believing.

Let us begin. Applying this to your body: The presiding intelligence in you, your intellect, sends this *idea of perfection* or *substance* from God to that part of your body in need. Yes, your intellect now sends this idea from your head very much like the telephone system. Then your central or *subconscious receives* (what your *intellect has grasped*) from God. This *idea* is *God's Word* for perfect function for that part of your body. It has now become your *definite thought* about that part, making it *your word*, too. So, even though previously the message from the race has been that you are weak in a certain part of your body—now the message has come to you in accordance with the Bible, "Let the weak say, I am strong"—(*there* by means of *God's substance idea*).

By like token, the same works in your human relations—if your intellect, through our "get together," now begins to send God's *substance idea for harmony* in your human relations down into your subconscious. As a matter of fact, it will then automatically begin to relay God's Way into your outer human relations. And remember, "For as the heavens are higher than the earth, so are My Ways higher than your ways—and My *thoughts* than your *thoughts*."

The same works for your prosperity and success. Increase in *God's substance idea* here reminds you, "I am the Lord thy God that teacheth thee to profit and leadeth thee in the way that thou shouldest go."

If you are really serious and quite willing, through your faith you have laid hold of *God's substance ideas*—His ideas of perfect function, harmony and increase—and they will now break through for you. Yes, from the God idea of perfect function to its result in your body. From the God idea of harmony to a literal transformation in your human relations. From the God idea of increase actually to witnessing this happening in your financial affairs.

But to ensure this, I have to explain four things here: FIRST, there has to be the *necessary response* to that *particular portion of substance* we need.

SECOND, this is *built up by meditating* upon that particular idea, which I trust you have already been doing with me. So it is taking over. That is a strong part of letting it happen.

THIRD, this meditating must be concluded by *decreeing* that substance idea—remembering that the quickest way to feel this substance idea is *to speak it*. So we are going to do just that.

FOURTH, *act it out*. Yes, "Act as though I were, and thou shalt surely know I AM." Acting it out is the strongest suggestion known to the subconscious.

Therefore I am going to ask you, if you will, to make these three decrees. One of them has to hit you where needed. I have asked you to meditate on this in a general way already. And you have been doing this. But now I would put it into an exact set of words for you: If it were in the body where you wanted this, say to yourself silently with me, "I decree the very *substance of life*. Its *substance idea for that part of my body* is now active in my personal subconscious. And my subconscious is now relaying that substance idea to the part of my body in need. It will not stop until its 'image and likeness' is in form or perfect function. And I expect results from this first treatment alone."

For your human relations, if that is the side in which you needed help, say, silently to yourself with me, "I decree the very *substance of love*, the *substance idea or know-how of God for my human relations*. This substance idea is now active in my personal subconscious. And my subconscious is now relaying that substance idea to where I need it most in my human relations. It will not be satisfied until it has taken over all the way into form, and I find myself acting it out. So the weak side of my human relations is being put right. And I expect results from this first treatment alone."

Finally, if it were your increase that was needed in the form of position, contacts, prosperity or whatever, say silently to yourself with me, "I decree that the very *substance of increase*, the *substance idea I need here for any and all of my insufficiencies*, is now active in my personal subconscious. And my subconscious is now relaying that substance idea to all the places in my affairs where I need increase. Also, the substance idea will not be satisfied until it is all the way into its forms of fulfillment, which I will witness. And I expect results from this first treatment alone."

There is one last thing you need to know—and it is all-important! What ENFORCES the IDEA—this substance idea—of God? You have been willing to respond to it, meditate upon it, decree it with authority and act it out. All of which serves one purpose—its entrance into your consciousness. That is done!

But there still remains the question, *"What enforces it?* Without understanding the answer to that question, you might think that the mere alignment of your consciousness up to the substance idea caused it to be enforced. No way! It is enforced—but not by you. It is enforced by its own Power. This is *God's very own Spirit*, with which you have been dealing. Therefore, it is ENFORCED *by the whole of that Spirit*. Remember the words "It is not I but the Father within [me]—He doeth the works!"

V

"CHILDREN, HAVE YE ANY MEAT [SUBSTANCE]?"

"Children, have ye any meat?" (John 21:5). Of course we understand that the question was not asking about physical food. Instead it is saying in our modern language, "I realize your consciousness has fallen a little, and we need to get it up again." How? Have you any *spiritual meat* or *idea* to chew on until you are back On High? Yes, the Higher Law of our nature is in full blossom for us right now if our consciousness is. As our consciousness drops, so does our hold on the Higher Law of our nature. We have the tendency to slacken up now and then. If we drop a little— things go down a little. If we come up again— so do the things. If our consciousness goes out completely, so do we, as far as this life plane is concerned. That is the way of the *Higher Law* of your nature and *your consciousness*.

A consciousness of God is not a grandiose, mystical thing. It is simply a vivid conviction of His presence right with us. A conviction of divine love. A conviction of divine ideas for all sides of our affairs. A conviction of divine power. A conviction of divine life. A conviction of divine supply. A conviction of divine order; and so forth.

Our mental conduct is the thoughts we think, the thoughts we feel and the thoughts we act out in words and deeds. Our proper mental conduct is not gazing fixedly at our solar plexus or rolling our eyes up—so that only the whites of our eyes show. When our consciousness has fallen a little, then things begin to go wrong. The human mind thinks it is somebody else's fault—other people, the weather, the government, or as a last resort —even God.

At our present stage of unfoldment, we see life through a "glass darkly"—but life really is not like that. If you looked out of your house through the old-fashioned glass panes—which you will remember were warped—the world outside would seem warped. But it would be the windowpane that was at fault—not the world.

When we are not feeding on *spiritual food substance*—when we do not have *spiritual meat substance* from the deep within of our souls to eat, meaning *right ideas or substance* about ourselves from God to chew on—our consciousness goes down and out.

In science: when our molecules move rapidly, we have heat. When our molecules move slowly, we have cold. This is a good analogy to *evil. It is life slowed down*. Sickness is the absence of the fast-moving molecules of ideas for life. Poverty is the absence of the fast-moving molecules of ideas for service and belief in supply "sufficient and to spare." Sadness is the absence of the fast-moving molecules of ideas for joy and a sense that it is great to be alive. Stupidity is the absence of the fast-moving molecules of ideas that come from knowing that God is our Mind, and that our brain is simply His instrument—so that we do everything easily and well.

Spiritual treatment is your means of stepping up the molecules of *ideas from God* for whatever side of our lives needs help. It is a law of life that we grow in the direction of the kind of *meat or idea we eat of, or dwell on*—in the privacy of our own thought. The Bible tells us what this *meat* is: "Ye shall know the Truth [*idea*], and the Truth [*idea*] will make you free." Yes, when *we come to feel it again*. It does not say a word about trying to put your body in the shape of a pretzel. It does not say anything about trying to scratch your left ear with the big toe of your right foot. Some people think, though, that such exercises are a short-cut to heaven. No, they are simply good physical exercises!

The Bible points out clearly what it is that *counts spiritually* when it asks, "Children, have ye any meat?" Yes, what do you dwell on in your *thought*? In the presence of a sick person, for example. In the presence of lack of position, or a position one is unhappy in—just a "bread and cheese" job to that person. The Bible tells us, "Ye shall know the Truth [idea], and the Truth [idea] will make you [him] free"—from the sickness, from the poverty, from the lack of position, from any such frustration. Yes, *when such knowing becomes your feeling again*.

Here is a treatment of Truth for position or true place of service: "A spiritual being cannot be out of his true place. I am a spiritual being—not just a human being. Who is in charge of a spiritual being's affairs? Only God! God is now completely in charge of my affairs, and step by step I am being led to my true place, which is already prepared for me by God." (In between treatments "turn out" or "reverse" any negatives.) When this *awareness* becomes a *conviction*, you will have the *consciousness* to receive your position.

Let me give you a powerful treatment for the healing of your body; and if there is a time gap or delay in getting results when you speak the Word for healing, remember that the limitation is of your own making—and not in it. So, if you are ready, this is a *practice* that will overcome the *time gap* or *delay* in the demonstration of the healing Word of God when you decree it—the Word of God being that office in God which takes the wholeness God has already prepared for your case and puts it at the other end *in you*: "God is Supreme Perfection for that side of your life. His Word is like unto that perfection. It takes cognizance only of that perfection. When you realize this perfection and make your decree from that plane of understanding, the Word goes forth through you and establishes that which is. It does not heal anything, because in its perfection there is nothing to heal. Its office is to behold and carry out the perfection of its being. Thus, he who realizes most thoroughly that God is that supreme perfection and speaks from that realization with conviction—will cause all things in his body to arrange themselves in divine order with the least delay."

In dealing with another person with whom you are having difficulties in human relations— do not accept the situation at its face value. In other words, do not evaluate it on that level, but be spiritually determined as a Truth student to change and improve it just as you would with sickness or lack. Some Truth students practice their Truth in illness or lack but not in human relations. To change or improve a human-relations situation: "Begin your spiritual treatment by seeing the Divine Spark, a Spark you would see become a flame in the other person. Do not pretend that he does not have the negative outer traits— but treat. Remind yourself that Divine Power to correct and redeem lives in that person as well as in yourself. Next, admit that Jones and I are not getting on—but I am handling it. Thus, I am the *adult* in this situation, and he is the *adolescent*;

and I am helping him over this phase through which he is passing."

To get results it sometimes takes two weeks, sometimes a few hours—depending on the degree of your realization. The other fellow will go on acting as he usually does for a while—but not for long. Above all, *you must be open to the change for the better in yourself.*

Finally, to take still another approach to life with the necessary consciousness of substance ideas to receive it: bringing through increased supply. Be reminded that the Great Prophets of the Bible, who knew the Higher Law of Prosperity, always did the following: They entered into the silence and prayed and blessed the *substance idea at hand* on the invisible side of being—prayed and blessed it into form; and so must you. The key to feeling and realizing the *substance idea* for the purpose of increasing supply is to become God's Thought Word about it.

To do that: *"Ask with a keen, clear-cut thought of His living substance or know-how for prosperity coming into form as you need it; speak*

His Word of abundance with power and authority; and, 'So shall His Word be that goeth forth out of your mouth, it shall not return unto you void . . . but shall prosper in the thing where unto you send it.' *Conclude by expecting results 'pronto.' Get the feeling of having lavished the substance of supply or His know-how upon that side of your affairs.*"

To bring this vital material to an unforgettable conclusion, take this away with you: Boiled down, what it comes to is not treating the situation, but rather treating your idea of the situation—until all sense of futility is gone and only *God's substance idea* of the working out possesses you!

VI

IN THE DIRECTION OF EXPANSION,
WHICH WE MUST ALWAYS SEEK,
WHAT DO YOU WANT TO DO NEXT?

No matter how orderly our lives may seem to be, there is always room for improvement. I am sure we all would agree with that. Basically, then, we are going to consider planning out our lives in a new and better way. This improvement that we are going to seek amounts to being about our Father's business a little more than ever— that this new and better thing can happen.

The Bible tells us that we can do just that, if we follow the Law of Vision. So such is going to be uppermost in our minds with regard to what we want to work out—this Law of Vision. With it comes a sense of Power, wiping out any sense of frustration or helplessness.

Now the first text of instruction is from Isaiah, chapter 48: verse 17. And it is very important to have in mind here that which we would work out next. It represents a step upward for us. The text reads, "I am the Lord thy God which teacheth thee to profit, which leadeth thee [or taketh thee] by the way thou shouldest go."

Nothing could be more direct or practical than that—meaning that God, as we now let Him, is going to teach us what we need to make this a successful step upward. Not only will He teach us, but He will literally take us with His Power to this new end.

Overall, it means that we are about to let God, in this first bit of instruction, show us how to have harmony and peace, accomplish great things and overcome present waste in our lives. And there is a little bit of waste in all of us.

Profit is the main key word or polar word in this passage. And its real meaning is to get the things worthwhile in life. That which we are now working out, I am sure, means that something worthwhile about living shall come into our fold. People usually think of the word *profit* in this passage as meaning money. But that is just one department of life. Its real meaning is to get the things that are worthwhile in general. And what you are working out is one step further into things worthwhile.

Now we want to become very basic about what we are working out. Fundamentally, wishes come from God. If you have had this correct desire of yours for some time—and it is not just a passing fancy—you must know that God thinks you are ripe for it. So you must "get on board" and do something about it. You see, just to wish, and not to know its connection with God and thus how to use it—this is waste!

We might ask ourselves right here, "How is this profit to come?" All right, return and consider the first part of the instruction, "I am the Lord Thy God which teacheth thee. . . . " That is part of the profit. You are going to be taught. But not only taught; the passage goes on to say, " . . . which leadeth [or taketh] thee in the way thou shouldest go." There is the rest of your profit.

In other words, through our utter willingness, God is going to show each one of us how we can do it, and then take us there.

Another similar text of instruction to back this up is from Psalm 32: verse 8, "I will instruct thee and teach thee in the way thou shalt go." I think that is quite definite and concrete—"I will instruct thee and teach thee in the way thou shalt go." I like that. God is being very specific and concise with us. We who are in this study have been in the habit of making our religion too general and too vague.

Let me give you an example of this: Recently I had the pleasure of speaking to about 800 people in this field in Brooklyn, N.Y. I was joined by three other speakers. And I could not help but notice the content of the talks that were given. While beautiful and fine, the content was so general that the people in the audience were forced to pick out what would be helpful to them.

Not so with God. His instruction is so direct and personal: "I will instruct thee and teach thee in the way thou shalt go." Then these words are added—that multiply its relation to the reader a hundredfold—"I will guide thee with mine eye." Does that not give us something intimate and personal from God? I think so!

You know, sometimes in our study of meta-physics, we get the notion that God is more or less a cold Something or Other. I am finding that more and more this seems to be happening to Truth students.

This passage makes most clear that your welfare is dear to the great heart of God. That includes the thing which you would work out next. He is as interested in it as you are. The fact that you have the desire to do this is prompted by Him. He would furnish you with the follow-through now, if you would let Him. You see, this God of ours has all the qualities of personality except its limitations.

To put it another way, there is nothing a good mother would not do for you that God would not do—only infinitely more. Because He has infinite capacity.

You, of course, must fulfill the law. That means the law of working with God, which is the same as working with the larger portion of your own being—His individualized presence in you. The law, pertaining to your part in working with Him, means believing in this thing you would now do. Means turning to Him again and again relative to this thing until it is accomplished. Means working with Him to get done what He wants done through you, which always leads to a happier, better life than you have ever known.

Now, if you are willing really to believe this about the thing you are working out—that God is with you on it; if you are willing to turn to Him often, starting today about it, you may fall down now and then, but you will still be trying because you know the relationship. You know that you are not alone. You know that you can be helped here. You know that the way can be eased for you—as only God can do it!

So once again consider the promise—how personal it is: "I will guide thee with mine eye" about that thing which you would work out. I think that is about as personal as it can get. Yes, it is personal to the nth degree.

I dwell upon this because I have found that some students of Truth seem to get the notion, since they are so sophisticatedly advanced in metaphysics, that God is more or less like the law of gravity.

In the very large work I built in Miami, I had a number of teachers under me and they still had things to work out. That is part of their growth. I was helped by giants in this field as I grew up in it—through private conversations, in which I was enabled to eradicate certain little kinks in my knowledge. So, in turn, one of my teachers in Miami came to me privately and said, "I think I have this correct. God is like the law of gravity, isn't He?" And I said, "Sorry, the analogy is a poor one."

The law of gravity is a law in the universal scheme of things in God. But it is just one item. To think of God as being like the law of gravity is ridiculous. The law of gravity always works for you, if you work with it. However, the law of gravity can never personally care about you. Frankly, it does not give a hang. It is an impersonal law. God is not like that. God personally cares about you. That is the vast difference!

Now we are going to come right down to where we are. This is from Proverbs, chapter 16: verse 9. It reads: "A man's heart deviseth his way. . . . " Nothing could be more clearly said. Each one of us in his own heart has devised what he needs to work out next. And it has come from within you, the depths of you. You must get over the notion that it just happened. If it has been with you for some time—not just a passing fancy—it means that it is there from God, to be made manifest through you. It means that God thinks you are ripe to handle this. To work with Him about it.

And so the first part of this says that your own heart deviseth your way, " . . . but the Lord directeth his [your] steps." You see, this wish that you have for a worthwhile working out in your life is there for a reason. We all want, generally, things like peace and health and greater abundance. And in some cases we want unique things. That is what you are after right now: things you really want to take place. To you, they mean more worthwhile living than you have ever known. Things deep, that you want to see through into manifestation—with God's help.

Now here is the Bible promise, and it adds these words, which we have already quoted: "A man's heart deviseth his way"—it has come up quite naturally from deep within him "but the Lord directeth his steps" with regard to that thing which has come from his heart. So specifically it means for you: "as to how," "as to when," and "as to place," will this desire work out in your life. Yes, that definite!

Men and women have the notion that they must bring this about themselves. The Bible is stressing here that you and I do not have to find the way ourselves. The reason this world is so full of disappointment is because so many of us think we have to find our own way. And then force ourselves to that point with will power. Of course, we can do that to a degree. But in time it turns sour in our hands.

However, when the Lord God is permitted to work in and through us and take us to His working out—not only will you be left with a good taste in your mouth, but also your life forever afterward will be changed for the better. So I ask that you ponder these words, and take them seriously: " . . . but the Lord directeth his steps." Are you willing that this happen?

Then, again from Isaiah, chapter 42: verse 16—like all Hebraic writings, it repeats itself for emphasis. It says it one way, and then repeats it another. So now it is saying it again in a different way: "I will bring the blind by a way they know not." "Blind" meaning you, because you do not know the way. I will bring you by a way that right now you know not. This I will do for you. And then it goes on to say, " . . . in paths that they have not known." Yes, by paths of which you are completely unaware right now. And again, "I will lead them." Meaning *I will take them*. Also, "I will make darkness light before them." How personal can you get! All the darkness about how to work this thing out. Eliminate that, by light, which will now show you the way.

Let us put it this way. Suppose at present you were confused about yourself. You could not think of a single way out of your predicament. Well, these promises are saying but one thing: "THERE IS A WAY! AND I WILL TAKE YOU DOWN ITS LANE. I WILL MAKE DARKNESS LIGHT ALL ALONG THAT LANE. MORE THAN THAT, I WILL MAKE THE CROOKED PLACES STRAIGHT, WHERE YOU HAVE BEEN ALL TWISTED UP."

So God is being very emphatic here. He is saying, "I will not just shift it around—your pain."

As someone has said, "A shift of pain is sometimes a relief." It may be a relief, but it is no answer. God is not saying that. With God, there is more to it than that. The Action of God will simply melt away the darkness with His own light in your consciousness.

And for emphasis, the Bible promises close here with this reminder, showing you how real and sincere they are: "These things will I do unto them, and not forsake them."

In these passages of instruction we now turn from the Psalms and Proverbs and Isaiah, and words are put into our own mouths—as though we were now ready to respond. What follows is found in Jeremiah, chapter 10: verse 23. Consider it carefully, for here you are speaking back to God: "O Lord, I know the way of man is not in himself . . . but the Lord will direct his steps." This is you—responding to God.

It is like I say to people sometimes: "In your prayers, why do you try to tell God how to do it? If you knew how to do it in the first place, why did you even pray? When you are really praying, it means that you do not know the way, that you

want God to open up the way." This is what
Jeremiah is having us do here—admitting something that we should in prayer: "O Lord, I know
that the way of man is not in himself . . . but the
Lord will direct his steps."

When I come to a point like this, I am always
reminded of a lady in this field, a student. It is
such a crystal-clear case. The thing she wanted to
work out next was a business of her own. This
meant a worthwhile kind of life into which she
fitted, so she thought. And I want to tell you, she
got that business of her own, and she was very
successful in it. But after a year of having it,
something happened to her. She simply stopped
treating or praying. To use her own words, she
thought she could "swing it herself." So she lost
that momentum with God.

None of us should let any department or activity in our lives go without prayer. All of us
who are really in this study should be continually
asking, in a sense, that God have every freedom
to come in and tidy us up where we need it.

While I am making this point, I might add
this: We should guard against any "Bluebeard's

room" in our castle—just like the little boy who was trying to find candy in the house. Mother knew when he was getting a little chair and getting on the table trying to reach for it. As she started for him, he yelled out, "Tay there, Tay there; don't come here!" There is a little bit of that in us all. Ask yourself, "Is there any area in my life, a 'Bluebeard's room,' in which I want to keep things the way they are—with no interference from God?" It could prove interesting!

There is an easy way of finding out. How? Listening to Truth lectures. If they are pleasant, we love them. But if by chance one of the lectures challenges us about a certain side of life, we usually wish a friend could have been there, and we usually add, "Joe could really have used this" or "This is just the thing for Mary—if she could only have been here!" This is really a way of "passing the buck." It could be a "Bluebeard's room" in your life.

We began this with something tremendous. A matter of whether we are willing to let this happen: The Lord, our God, will not only teach us how to work this thing out, but also will literally

take us to the working out! And in doing this—
being willing to let God take over here—we are
leading a consecrated life. Yes, a consecrated life
is *living along these lines*. And I am going to pin-
point them for you.

First, recognize this good desire that is in
you—came from God. While you have conceived
in your heart that it is there, He thinks you are
ripe for it—ready to work with Him there. Let
it come to that triumphant conclusion. That is
first!

Second, will you continue your willingness
now, and be willing to let God interpret your
desire? *Third*, will you be willing to let Him
make the necessary contacts for you? *Fourth*, will
you be willing to let Him give you the power or
steam to get there, and beyond that, added
energy, considering that this new adventure is going to take more out of you? *Fifth*, will you be
willing to let Him provide the increased supply
that may very well be needed to consummate
this? And *sixth*, will you be willing that He open
all the doors, so that without great stress and
strain through trying blindly by yourself the way

may open for you and you may do it with ease? If so, you must give your desire back to God for each of these—AGAIN AND AGAIN!

I think I have you to the point where this has become real. Where you feel that God loves you. That He is intimately interested in this next thing you would work out. That He wants to be let in on it with you.

So I am now going to tell you a couple of true stories to make you realize how much God can help you here.

One is about a man who listened to a talk of this nature. He had always wanted to be a writer. Nothing odd about that—many people do. But it was a very strong desire with him, over a long period. And he remembered from this talk that he had this desire. That his own heart had devised it. That he now had to have it interpreted. What would he write about? And he really began to pray about it. He was *inspired* to run his fingers through the Bible looking for a passage that might give him the idea for a good novel.

Such is not unusual. Many of our great novels have been written from a single passage in the Bible. He came upon his, and he was so inspired by it that he wrote a novel. Then he went out to the various publishers, but no one would handle it. So he went back to the lecturer he had heard tell about this and said to him, "This is ridiculous, because I really opened myself to God and He interpreted my feeling for writing. He led me to this passage, and from it I wrote this novel."

And the lecturer said, "Well, you are like the man who couldn't see the tree for the forest. You have done the second step that you needed—the interpretation. You were shown the passage, and you had a wonderful idea for a novel. But on the third step—the contacts for it—you stopped. You tried to "swing it alone." You did not follow through in your willingness. Go back home and start praying for contacts before you go out and make the rounds of publishers again."

The man did. Went the same round of publishing houses, and one of them now accepted his novel—the *second time* around. The first time— no! In other words, something was now made to happen that otherwise was not there. And it turned out to be a best-seller! That is an interesting—also a true—story.

The second true story is so meticulous and so exacting, that the working out of God's answer for the person is almost stupefying. This lady was a commercial artist, an amateur, but a very good one. She illustrated children's books as a pastime. She had a desire within herself, though, to do it professionally. Her "own heart devised" that.

She heard this kind of Truth talk also, and she realized that contacts was what she needed next. So she began really to pray about contacts for an opening—to be a professional in commercial art, specifically in children's books.

This, that follows, is the story she told me: She lived in Boston. Having first prayed about contacts, she went downtown, on the day her club met, to do two things at one time. She did her shopping, then went to the hotel and appeared at the door of her club with her packages. She stood in the doorway and then started to go in—but she did not recognize a single soul. There was a whole new group of people. It dawned on her that she had miscued: This was not the day to do her shopping, and not the day of her club. It was another club, and another group of people.

She started to beat a retreat with all of her packages, but the people on the speaker's platform beckoned to her. She looked around, and there was no one behind her, so she thought they must be waving for her to come in for some reason. She went in, and they made a big fuss over her. Finally all was clarified. It seems they thought she was their speaker. She, of course, was not. But she looked so much like their speaker, she could have passed for her twin sister.

Well, they were so interested in her because of the resemblance, they insisted she stay. So she put down her packages and waited, and the real speaker came in shortly afterward. They told the speaker briefly what had taken place, and she said, "She does look like me, and I play hunches. You just stay right there until I get through." She then gave her speech. She was an executive from New York, head of a department in a big company there.

Then she sat down with my friend, and again she said, "I play hunches, and there must be a reason for this. What do you do?" My friend said, "Well, I am sort of a commercial artist. As an amateur I do all kinds of children's booklets. I should really like to do it on a larger scale, professionally."

The lady speaker then said, "That is very strange. My hunch is coming true here—the reason for this happening. I am the head of a department, and we have put in an additional program for children now. We are really looking and scouting for top talent. I am going to say there is a reason why I met you—and your talent. I will write to you."

She went back to New York and wrote to my friend, saying, "This is what I want you to do. My assistants will send you books, and they will say what kind of illustrations they want done. But you will do them your own way. Submit them, and we shall see."

So my friend received these books. She illustrated them and sent them back. And she won a position with this firm in New York—without even having to go out from her house. She worked at home illustrating the books there. Truly a beautiful arrangement!

Now I want to say this to you: How could anyone get all that together by himself? This is what we must now be doing. The essential thing on her part, *as on our part*, will be the spiritual willingness to take the next step necessary in our case— in mind (first) through prayer—and it probably is INTERPRETATION and then CONTACTS.

Then do the same for the power or steam to get there—as well as added energy. Then do the same for additional supply. Then do the same for all doors opening easily. If we have the willingness to see all these stages through with God, then we may say with Isaiah, "HERE AM I; SEND ME" (Isaiah 6:8).

Now such is a fitting conclusion to all that we have done—if you are willing enough.

I may say this in closing: "Is it not amazing how much treasure lies in the Bible?"

VII

WOULD WE NOT ALL LIKE TO SHATTER
OUR WORLD TO BITS AT TIMES, AND
PUT IT BACK TOGETHER ACCORDING TO
OUR HEART'S DESIRE?

I want you to have the sense that you have really used the important information of this subject before I get through. Yes, I want you to feel that you have used it up!

In this country we believe in getting things done. You know, rather than just sitting around and moaning about conditions. We have built, for instance, some remarkable dams which have rehabilitated acres and acres of barren wasteland. By like token, the study of Truth is doing this to the barren patches in our own lives. We Truth students are not just sitting down, dropping a tear and blaming it upon people, conditions and situations—and, when we run out of them, even God.

We have a remarkable passage on which this

particular material is based: "Ho, everyone that thirsteth, come ye to the waters . . . " (Isaiah 55:1). So, if you feel that things are getting a little bit *deserty*, the whole point here is to turn on the eternal waters of Spirit. This subject is dedicated to getting things done in the direction of remaking your world. How? The thing to do is to lay on this water—the water of the eternal Spirit of God.

Here is the first key: *Think differently than the form of thought that brought on your drought.* Let me repeat that. Think differently than the form of thought that brought on your drought. Yes, if your body has been in a challenging situation or your human relations or business—think differently than the form of thought that brought about the condition.

You see, the kingdom of God itself can be within your thinking there. As Jesus put it, "The kingdom of heaven is within you." Therefore, you have the privilege of thinking directly from the kingdom of heaven *instead* of the way you have been thinking. It does not matter what the difficulty might be, change your thinking—to

thinking from heaven or *the God-plan for you*.
Yes, change your thinking to that, and keep it
changed!

The Bible tells us, "Many are the afflictions
[even] of the righteous"—yes, those who try to
live rightly—"but the Lord, [the Higher Law of
God] delivereth them out of all." That promise
is given us in Psalm 34: verse 19. You know,
sometimes people get the notion that as soon as
they adopt this teaching they will have no more
problems. Of course, that is ridiculous. There
will always be new ones. They are the means by
which we grow. Then, too, we all have considerable baggage from out of our past—some of
which we carried over. After all, when you came
into this plane, there was no customs inspector
present.

So these things come up, things we have not
yet worked out. Yes, eventually they come up.
And that is all right. Now that we are in Truth,
we welcome them. We just clear them up, and
they never come back again.

In Psalm 37: verse 4 we are told, "Delight thyself also in the Lord," this Higher Law of God,

this Plan of God, "and He shall give thee the desires of thine heart." This is one of the greatest single passages in the Bible. "Delight thyself also in the Lord," the Higher Law of God, the Plan of God for you, "and He shall give thee the desires of thine heart." I don't know of a more practical verse in the entire Bible, a more practical verse for getting things done in our lives right now in the remaking of our world.

Let us face ourselves frankly. As long as we are worried about things in our lives, we cannot be giving ourselves wholly to God. There can be no delight in us, as long as we are worried. No matter how long we have been in Truth.

Then, too, as long as we practice any form of spiritual resignation—resign ourselves to some negative condition—we are not giving ourselves wholly to God. So no more of that.

Even going to God with a sense of bounden duty is not enough. Of course, however you go to God is helpful. But going to God only out of a sense of bounden duty is not good enough. This is what the Bible is seeking to bring home to us through this passage.

This is actually a staggeringly important text. You and I as Truth students should bring it to our attention at least once a year. It is that important! "Delight thyself also in the Lord," that Higher Law, His Plan, "and He shall give thee the desires of thine heart." You know, if we really believed that—all the men would throw their hats into the air. And what the women would do, I don't know.

Let us put it in terms of something we can see quite clearly. If a big financier gave you his word to finance you to the tune of a few thousand, you would believe him, correct? So why not God? He promises much, much more here. "Delight thyself also in the Lord; and He shall give thee the desires of thine heart."

But, of course, there is an *if*. And the *condition* is, if we "delight ourselves also in the Lord." Yes, if we go to God with regard to any condition in our lives—with a sense of sheer delight. It amounts to this: I am conditioned through my study to know that I have at my disposal all that God is. Thus I turn to Him with delight—sheer joy. After all, if you had made a mistake while driving, gone nine miles out of your way, but had a good car—you would think nothing of it. All of which is a good analogy to the one who knows his God and delights in turning back to God for any correction, for any replacement, for any straightening out in his life.

Of course, this requires something of us! "Delight thyself also in the Lord" means *thrilling to the Truth* that God is there in all His Power, cares for us personally and brings results pronto! But watch out for the devil here. He is always right at hand because he is only the old in-a-rut you. He usually has this to say: "Well, He didn't answer your last prayer, you will remember." But just toss him out unceremoniously, you see; just throw him out.

Now the "desires of your heart," this great promise says, will be brought into form. The desires of your heart at this particular time in your life means what you *really* want to happen in your affairs. And you know, we all do quite a bit of bluffing, even with ourselves, about the desires of our heart. But this particular promise is saying to us, "The party of the first part, God, guarantees to the party of the second part, you, the 'desires of your heart.'" Yes, the satisfactory working out of whatever your deepest wishes may be.

The next verse is a follow-through of it, Psalm 37: verse 5. It continues your *requirements* or your *ifs*. Remember, it is a follow-through of the first, and the first is what? "Delight thyself also in the Lord; and He shall give thee the desires of thine heart." The follow-up passage is, "Commit thy ways unto the Lord; . . . " the Higher Law, the Plan God has for you. "Commit thy ways. . . . " Your ways up to now have left you short. Here have the sense of opening up everything within yourself to God's higher ways. "Trust also in Him; . . . " These are the *ifs*, the *conditions* of the promise. Now if yours is a "delight" in the Lord, and you "commit" all your ways unto the Lord and then "trust" that He is now on the job working out your heartfelt desire—" . . . He shall bring it to pass."

We might ask ourselves, how do we commit?—assuming that ours is a real delight in going to God. Thus we have the proper atmosphere within ourselves. How do we commit this completely to God? Well, think *first of all* that whatever you need, God will supply it—as simple as that. Once that is certain within you, then " . . . trust also in Him."

Let me remind you of an analogy I used before: If you had an electric range and you wanted to cook something, you would turn it on. Then you would trust the electric heat to do the cooking. You would not stand by, grit your teeth, clench your fists and try to make the food cook. You would simply trust the electric heat to do its job.

The same is true in Truth. You know that there is not any need you have that God will not fulfill. So go to Him in sheer delight, commit the work needed to be done completely to Him, and then trust that He is going to bring it about. Of course, *you will do the things that come to you in the outer*, just like anybody else; but you will have so much more going for you from God.

You are now a branch hooked back up to its trunk again, and the sap of God begins to flow. His Holy Spirit now carries its substance or knowhow by means of Its Word to the spot where needed in you. Yes, writes itself into "your inward part." You will do in the outer anything that comes to you to do. But you are mindful, "I am the manifesting nature, He is the work." As that manifesting nature, you let His will be done.

"His ways are higher than your ways as the heavens are above the earth." In committing your heartfelt desire to Him, you are opening up all of your consciousness "to His ways"—then trusting in them with utter belief that you are on the road out; that the things you now do, the things you now say, the things you now act out—will all be from Him.

Just for a moment, let us come back to ourselves—the way we factually are. Be really honest. You know, of course, that you have no real enemies. You are in Truth, so you know that for sure. You have no real enemies except those within yourself. Something in you—that has been apart from God—has brewed the seeming outer enemies and attracted them to you.

Whatever comes to us, then, in the form of a person or condition or thing that is untoward— something in us attracted that. So the enemy is within. Thus we are taking time to delight in the Truth that we can turn to our God—commit this side of our lives to Him—and trust Him to straighten it out and bring it back to spiritual "par."

Now we have the sense that we are back on the spiritual beam—the High Road. That all this of God is jelling within us. That we are going to be truly His manifesting nature for a wonderful working out. Face honestly, though, the fact that nothing can come to us that does not find correspondency in our mentalities. I have already said that. But we must admit to it. And we must open ourselves completely to His higher ways to be straightened out.

Face it! The only thing that stands in our way to this working out must be ourselves. Now if we can see that, we can let ourselves be healed. If someone else did the things we do to ourselves— the mistreatment of our bodies, things we fear, things we say about ourselves—we would be most indignant. Yet this is precisely what has been the bottleneck!

Somebody else can pull a tooth for you, but no one can speak for you *permanently*. A practitioner can help you only *temporarily*. Basically,

you must get around to that decreeing yourself.
Ever stop to think about that? No one can really
speak for you permanently. Now in this
challenge, whatever it may be, you are going to
speak something to it. And you are going to have
a new evaluation of this speaking for all the
things that you have to meet in the future.

The Bible tells us in Job 22: verse 28, "Thou
shalt also decree a thing, and it shall be established unto thee." Be mindful again, no practitioner can speak for you permanently. Think
about it. It is most challenging. Especially when
you think of the negative aspects of such
speaking—the criticism, the pessimism, the negation that, to some degree, you have decreed. You
know what is going to happen there. You must
know, being in the Truth. As long as you are with
this pessimism, this criticism, this negation—you
are going to manifest its results.

All right, we are done with that! You will need
a sense of humor here. You see, if someone else
were doing this to you on a regular basis—being
pessimistic, being negative, being critical—you
would go looking for him with a lethal weapon.
That is, if you were not in the study of Truth.

The big point here is, when you find yourself outside of the kingdom of heaven—begin to treat yourself *like someone you love*. Get yourself back into the fold.

I am going to give you a little technique that I use myself: I always think of my subconscious— let me clarify this first, because we have people of different backgrounds and different movements studying with us. I have no quarrel with equating the Universal Subconscious with God. But I have a lot to say when you assume to equate the ability of your personal subconscious with God. God created you to work directly upon your subconscious, and from there up onto the canvas of your conscious mind—then out into your world. But through your free will, your subconscious has become a far cry from being such a meeting ground for the will of God.

Here is my technique: I always think of my personal subconscious as being about seven or eight years of age—and not too bright at that. Why? Because it cannot think for itself. It can only carry out. It is simply a reflex action part of your brain. That is all it has ever been. It has taken on what God has put into it plus what you

and the race have put into it—and it conducts itself accordingly—that is all. When you start giving it accolades, the main one you *can* give to it
is—that it carries out anything you personally
have come to believe. But it can never distinguish
between good and bad. So it carries out either
good or evil in keeping with what you have come
to believe.

Thus I treat my subconscious the way a firm
parent would treat her child. This is the way I
talk to it, and you might like it for your own use.
Now let us say I have been in some kind of
trouble, some kind of "mishmash"—things have
not been going well. Instead of talking out here,
I talk to myself, which is all right just so long as
you don't let anyone see you. This is what I say,
speaking to my subconscious: "This has to stop—
right now. And this is why: *I can't afford the
punishment.*" That is exactly the way I talk to it.
"This has got to stop. And this is why: *I can't afford the punishment.*" Try it!

I am going to show you how this works. I will
use a person of note to illustrate it: You know that
Edison was partially deaf. And it was said he
sometimes felt he was better off. Why? Because
he did not have to hear all the silly things that

were going on. But your personal subconscious is never deaf. Do you know what it is always doing? It is always listening to you. To see if you have something interesting to say—and to be carried out.

What have you been saying recently about yourself? "What a mess my life is." "There is no way out." "Every door has turned against me," and so forth. This is outrageous, of course. Your subconscious being very impersonal, you see, accordingly reacts like this: "Dear old Joe upstairs—wants some more doors closed on him. He wants things to get worse. He wants the mess to get messier." Which is exactly what it then carries out. Remember, it cannot even think—being only a conditioned-reflex portion of the brain; it can only carry out.

So it is always listening—to see if you have something interesting to say. And I propose that you get yourself a new start. That you really begin to have something to say to your subconscious that is in keeping with God's plan.

Let me give you another illustration to help you. It has to do with Paderewski, the great pianist. It is the story of Paderewski and the stone-deaf man. It seems that the idiosyncrasies of Paderewski were prominently on display just before his concert—as usual. Prior to getting down to the business of playing, he would always exhibit them first. He would sit down. Then he would take out a handkerchief and dust things. They were already immaculate, but he would dust them anyway. Go over everything, dust the chair and the whole thing. Finally, he would change his "tails" a little bit, and move around some more. It was quite an act.

Now remember, you have a stone-deaf person attending his first concert given by Paderewski. And the stone-deaf person is watching all this. After ten minutes the stone-deaf fellow was quite bored. To him, you see, Paderewski was funny for a while—but he began to repeat the same idiosyncrasies. Instead of playing, he started all over, going through his little act—building himself up to play.

We are like that in our idiosyncrasies or negative habits. While we are having fun with Paderewski, let us turn it on ourselves. Frankly, we are really a *riot* to watch. And we ought to develop a sense of humor about our peculiar negative habits of thinking. You know—our criticising, our resenting, our fearing an outcome that has not happened yet—any of these tendencies. If someone else did this we would say, "He will not get away with it. It will come home to roost." And this is, of course, equally true of ourselves. We will not ever get away with it. It will always come home to roost.

So begin to ridicule your own idiosyncrasies. Have a spiritual sense of humor about them. Learn to laugh at them. There is nothing that throws out old negative habits quicker. Then they put their tails between their legs and scoot away. So the next time you find yourself going through your negative paces, I want to give you a little picture that you can't forget: I want you to think of a cow chewing her cud. Will you do that? At least the cow is digesting her food according to her instincts. What cud are you chewing? That is the point! The cow, you see, has an excuse for the appearance of monotonously chewing her cud. She does it by instinct and for good digestive purposes. What about you? What excuse have you for the cud you are chewing by habit?

If you can get that picture of a great big cow chewing her cud, you may help yourself. After all, you know, we men and women are a part of

the species called man, and with that species
comes a great inheritance. We are a higher creation than all the lesser creatures on earth, and
we owe them something. We are here to give
them spiritual dominion, not silly habits.

The fact is that with our equipment, we can
form concepts, and lesser creatures cannot. That
ability is always with us. Yes, we can form our
own concepts. But that can be a curse or it can
be a blessing. The person that is lost in criticising,
being pessimistic, being negative, has formed
those concepts and is living with them. However,
there is no one who cannot reform his own concepts. And when he does, he turns what has been
his curse into a great blessing.

So, friends, let us leave this material determined to stop bringing curses down upon our
heads, stop being the bottleneck to our own good.
Let us leave—spiritually determined to begin
releasing, peculiar to our needs, the blessings of
heaven. These blessings of heaven, if they are to
reach us, *must begin to be a part of our thinking*!

We must begin to think from what we belong
to in God rather than from pessimism, from negation, from criticism and so forth. We must be-

gin to think of what belongs to us in the kingdom of heaven and therefore what belongs to us here on earth—and gently insist upon it! This must become our new standard of thinking. We must make a central theme of the following: Pick out everything we dislike about ourselves, and start reforming those concepts. Yes, begin to think from the kingdom of heaven for the body, for human relations, for supply, for justice, for protection, for whatever. Then that thinking becomes our own. And this new kind of thinking is solidified within us by *acting it out*. Why? Because acting it out is the strongest suggestion known to the subconscious.

There is nothing on this good earth that you could do that would better enable you to begin to get things done in your world. Get things done by remaking your world section by section. Yes, you tuning in to *a new kind of thinking* from God—that you belong to Him, and what belongs to Him, belongs to you!

Now I want to build this up in you. I want everyone having read this to come away with the sense that he has actually placed his own personal life, every side of it, under Higher Law or the Plan of God for man. We know that the essence of Truth is to repeal every lesser law we have been under—by placing ourselves under Higher Law in our thinking, feeling and acting.

We are going to start by doing this spiritual treatment very carefully together. Let us begin: "I claim for myself that I am now in the Presence of God's pure Being at the central-most part of my own person. I am mindful that *the door opens inward* to all that I belong to in God. This is my *new world*. This is the 'life more abundant.' In turning the door that opens inward, I am doing it with a sense of *sheer delight*. I am not doing it just because I should. I am not doing it out of bounden duty. Rather I am doing it with a sense of sheer delight. From this moment I am going to think only from God's pure being. I am now going *to think* only from health and wholeness. I am now going *to feel* only from health and wholeness. And I am now going *to act* only as though this new health and wholeness were becoming me.

"Again I claim that I am in the Presence of God's pure Being, that mine is *utter delight*, as I now turn the *door that opens inward* and take on peace for my mind and harmony for my affairs. I am now going *to think* only from this peace and harmony. I am now going *to feel* only from this peace and harmony. I am now going *to act* as though only this peace were taking possession of my mind and this harmony were flowing into my affairs.

"Once more I claim that I am now in the Presence of God's pure Being. I have opened the *door that opens inward*. And I have done this with *utter delight*—utter delight in His Higher Law for my prosperity and success. So I am now going *to think* only from this increased prosperity and success. I am now going *to feel* only from this increased prosperity and success. I am now going *to act* only as though this new prosperity and success were becoming me."

Thus you are back with God. You are thinking, feeling and acting only from Him. Nothing in this world can stop you from getting these things done—health, wholeness, peace, harmony, prosperity and success. Yes, nothing in this world can prevent you from getting these things done and *remaking your world* from within, because you have come to the "waters" of God's Holy Spirit and laid those "waters" onto your new world!

THE CENTERFOLD OF THIS BOOK

VIII

DO YOU NEED TO
WAKE UP THE POWER OF YOUR WORD?

I am going to tell you in advance that this will be the deepest kind of presentation of Truth that you are about to read. Its value is that it gives you the *clearest* kind of understanding of the Spirit of God and your ability to use the Spirit of God by speaking Its Word. Also the value of this particular material lies in the fact that we have always tried to speak the Word of God, but in this material you garner a whole new insight *as to what takes place from God as we speak His Word*. The whole mechanism that takes place is something *quite apart from you* except the fervor and the faith in which you declare the Word. Much help will be found in this particular *spiritual treatment* that I am about to give. It will be very pertinent to any special thing that you are working out at the moment. Much of the explanation will be given here.

Just sit back and think it through and seek to feel it. Feel how reasonable it is. It is not whimsical; rather, it is based upon an exact action—when you truly speak the Word of God. So, whatever you are working out right now, I want you to prepare yourself. You are going to place the Word of God in action for that working out. May I ask that you now change your position, wherever you are, and let your seat gather the full weight of your body. See how relaxed you can become. And close your eyes so that you are away from the world and totally lost in decreeing God's Word for your particular case. Now I ask that you gently consider the following and see just how reasonable your faith can become. When your faith becomes reasonable to you, it will become effective.

The Bible tells us, "In the beginning God, His Spirit. . . . " Where did that Spirit move? It moved upon the face of the waters, creating patterns for all things. And how relevant that is to the case of *man*. For "waters" in the Bible represent his feelings, his convictions, that lie in his subconscious and which rule his life. And you are asking the Word of God to feed into your subconscious just that which is needed at this moment. You are in the process of speaking the Word of God for your case, being open to the changing of patterns within your own subconscious through the Word of God. I want you to *feel* this with me. Thus the Spirit of God, containing its own self-knowingness through its substance *idea*, now makes things out of itself. Yes, by an inner act upon its own substance *idea*. And, when did that Spirit manifest? According to the Bible, as God spoke the Word, saying, "Let there be *this* and *that* and *this*." And remember, God created you in His own image and likeness to do the same, to speak God's Word to get things done in your life. Therefore Spirit, when you speak its Word in faith, believing, creates its own patterns for your help. How? By an inner act upon its own *substance idea*. Nothing from you. Yes, by an inner act upon its own substance idea. And then feeds that substance idea or know-how into your subconscious. *Feel* that beginning now!

Just as there is a *beginning of this action from God*, so there must be a *beginning of an action in you* to receive it. That must be an *inner act on your part* to receive this help. And that should be the act of *speaking God's Word in the absolute conviction* of this self-knowingness of Spirit to handle the case you have submitted to it.

Now, your belief should be reasonable to you, because it has become understanding faith. So, without further ado, have the sense that you are now *speaking God's Word*. Decree it about that spot in your life or that of another needing help. "Let there be . . . " and name here the fulfillment of that need as though it were already done. For in Truth—it already is. And in the silence that follows, let that *feeling* be yours.

Now this is quite a subject. How many of you would like to be able to speak God's Word and get better results than you ever had up to now? After all, why are you studying Truth? Would you be willing to go a little deeper than you have ever gone—in a way of explanation so that it becomes more reasonable to your mind what you should be doing? Would that appeal to you?

I am going to give you just a very few things to jot down in your mind. They will be very brief, and I am going to give them to you because you can chew on them at your leisure—go over them and over them. Each time you do, your faith will become more reasonable to you.

We are going to consider once more, "Wake Up the Power of Your Word." But, first, I want to share with you briefly a *preface* that I believe is very necessary:

Spiritual faith reaches beyond all reason on this plane to get its results. We all agree with that, don't we? Yes, *reaches beyond all reason to get its results*. However, *strangely enough* the word of spiritual faith demonstrates itself through us *when that kind of faith becomes reasonable to us*. Is that not strange? But true. The more reasonable this technique is within you, the more you use it. Yes, *the more it makes sense to you*. So, I pray to allow it to make sense for you.

Now, the Bible tells us that the day will come when all of us must learn to worship God in Spirit and in Truth. That is the deepest point of the Bible. Most of us have quoted it. Yes, when all the surface techniques go and we get down to what really counts, we will have finally learned to worship God in Spirit and in Truth.

Why is this so? When your faith becomes reasonable to you, it becomes effective. That is why! And your belief becomes reasonable when you know *what Spirit is and how it works*. Yes, that is when it becomes reasonable—when you know what Spirit is and how it works!

You have often heard me say that Holy Spirit is the means by which God acts through man. That is God's motivation, His way of working through you. Now I want you to memorize this simple little formula, so brief: "*Once we learn to be the channel for letting that Spirit change the cause in a person's life, we change the effect.*" Now listen to that again. Once we learn to be the channel for letting that Spirit change the cause in a person's life, we change the effect. Does that make sense?

I ask, then, that we let that be our *theme* for making our faith more reasonable, that it may become more effective. To continue that theme let us go back to the First Creative Principle as it was given in the Bible. "In the beginning God. . . . " Yes, in the beginning—His Spirit, right? Next, let me ask the question: Where did this Spirit move, according to the Bible? After all, the earth was without form and void. The Bible tells us that the Spirit of God moved upon the face of the waters. Will you remember that? And doing what? Creating patterns for all things. Yes, it moved upon the face of the waters *creating patterns for all things.* How relevant to the case of man, whose "waters" symbolize his feelings or convictions in his subconscious mind, where all causes for his life lie. Think about that. All causes for your life lie within your subconscious. These *feelings* are your "waters." How fitting, then, that Spirit can work upon the "waters" of you.

Now that you see this, I am going to seek at this moment to give you the deepest and clearest picture I know of how Spirit operates. So clear that you will see it as you use the Word. Just think, you are getting ready to "speak the Word," to release the Spirit of God. *This is a description of what happens from Spirit's side, or God's side,* of the work needed to be done.

So this is what happens *beyond* you. The Spirit of God, containing Its own self-knowingness, by Its substance *idea* makes things out of itself. Yes, through an inner act upon Itself, It changes the patterns in man.

Now let me just informally describe this to you again. You are beginning to speak the Word. You are then beginning to release something. The Spirit of God, containing Its own self-knowing-ness, now acts upon Its own substance idea for your case. Nothing to do with you; rather, Its own substance idea. What is the substance idea? The greatest thing that could ever happen to you in your case. This self-knowingness of Spirit acts upon Its own substance idea—and then begins to feed it to what? To your subconscious, where it is needed. Do you get the picture of this action? I purposely changed the wording here so that you might see it perhaps more clearly.

That is the action of Spirit. It is not the action of Mary or Henry or Sadie or anybody else. It is the action of Spirit. Now you want to know, on top of that, *your* part in the application of Spirit. And your part in the application of Spirit is simply an *inner act on your part*. An act of spiritual consciousness or conviction of what God is doing when you speak Its Word. *That is your part.* Do you follow that? It is an inner act on your part. An act of spiritual consciousness or conviction of what Spirit is doing as you speak Its Word.

Now, we have *two inner acts: God's inner act* and *your inner act.* They *both must happen* to have results out here. Will you remember this? It is paramount!

You see, this inner act on your part is *awareness, to the point of conviction, of the self-knowingness of Spirit*—and that should give you something real on your end. This inner act is an awareness, to the point of conviction, of the self-knowingness of Spirit now acting upon Its own substance idea and feeding that and putting that into your subconscious. *One of the greatest things to learn here is that God does not work directly on your body or your business or your human relations. He works directly on your subconscious.* Then the hand heals. Then the business changes. Then human relations change. The change is in your "water," in your subconscious. Will this help you in the future? Give you a vivid picture of what is taking place? You see, the causative life, Spirit, is within you. That is what we are saying. You have a right to it. It is within you to latch on to at anytime. That is why the Bible says, "Know ye not that ye are the temple of God, and that the Spirit of God dwelleth in you?" That means the causative Spirit of God is at hand—and ready and waiting to be used.

Once you know that the causative Spirit of God is right at hand with you, it should become reasonable to you to speak Its Word: *Yes, the causative Spirit of God is with me, but to get It into action there has to be an inner act on my part.* I must speak It with a deep conviction that this *self-knowingness of God will act upon Its own substance idea and put this in me.* Once I understand that, then it would seem reasonable for me to speak the Word.

Now, how many of you knew this already? Then, you have grown. Correct? However, you needed to boil it down. And you have!

Here, I am going to come to spiritual treatment itself, which is the hub of this teaching. You can hear about it 'til doomsday and read about it 'til doomsday. But sooner or later you are going to have to *learn* spiritual treatment. You hear much about meditation, and meditation has its place—a time of quiet. But there is no comparison between it and spiritual treatment—because spiritual treatment is specific. It goes right to the core, right to the thing, the thing at hand that you need done.

Let us get a real good picture of what happens to us when we go into spiritual treatment. I would suggest that you memorize this simple sentence: *Your spiritual treatment, either for self or another, is basically self-contemplation on your part of what Spirit is doing when you speak Its Word.* Don't you like that? And therefore there is not one of us here who cannot give this Word that we are talking about its own creative expression in his life. You have as much right to it as I have or a Jesus or a Moses or anyone else. This creative expression in which we seek to fit our case is the very Spirit of God boiled down to Its action on the case at hand. That is what we want always. *We want His action on the case at hand!*

Now, once we realize that there is such a Spirit within us, and that by Its Word we can transform our lives, there is joy past all finding out. Why? Because it means the overcoming of matter

—now and forever. That is what it should mean to you. Whatever the matter is, you can overcome it by an inner act of speaking the Word and releasing the action of God there.

Here, as you decide to do this—say, for your body or your business or your human relations—what begins to take place? The very Spirit of God and Its Word now become your mold and your vision for the healing of self and others. You know that as you make this inner act one of response to the act of God within, you are on the way to healing that nothing out here can supplant. More than that, it means that once you get onto this, the inner act releasing the action of God begins to make you into its mold and vision for prosperity. And, finally, this same inner act releasing the act of God begins to make you into its mold and vision for harmony for self and others.

Once we begin to use this Word, what are we doing? We are letting Spirit mold us into Its own vision, into Its own knowingness. How? By letting It act upon Its own substance idea and feed that to us, changing the patterns in our subconscious accordingly. As the Bible puts it, "I will write my laws into their inward parts." That is

what is taking place. Yes, as God begins to feed
to us, out of His own substance idea, what we belong to there—He is writing His higher law in our
inward parts.

Take a young person whose history has been
sickness. He gets into Truth, and he really begins
to believe that by an inner act he can release the
action of God and mold himself into a new
vision. Then he can have a new history of health.

Now, if we are going to do this, there is one
other picture that I must paint and make vivid.
Already you have had a clear description of how
God begins to work: His own self-knowingness
acts upon His own substance idea, and He then
feeds it into your subconscious. Nothing done by
you. He does it. The inner act on your part is to
have the kind of consciousness that believes—you
see? *An inner act that believes this can take place
through you*! That is what makes a Jesus, Moses,
Elijah, or Elisha.

Thus I have to paint this picture for you, if you
are going to let this happen in your life—so that
you can become a new mold and a new vision for
yourself, and even get it going for someone else
you want to help. This needs to be said. Other-

wise the information is lacking something. I say to you, let there be this *clear picture*:

Because the Spirit of God is an absolute intelligence all around us and in us, there must be an absolute consciousness by which to receive It. We are getting back to your inner act now, you see? Because this Spirit of God is an absolute intelligence all about you and in you, there has to be an absolute consciousness by which to receive It. That is what makes the difference between these great prophets and people who just go along in life and never discover it.

What we are saying here is that this cannot be, then, the consciousness of illness or poverty or disorder. I want you to have this absolute consciousness or feeling that the *Word with you is unconditioned*. I want you to have this absolute consciousness or feeling that the Word with you is unconditioned and unqualified in its ability to heal, to prosper, and to draw all men upward into their spiritual nature. Yes, I want you to have this absolute consciousness or feeling that the Word with you is unconditional and unqualified! Will you take that stand for yourself when you get to your spiritual treatment?

Your word is going to be unqualified, unconditioned by the world, because you know that if
you perform this inner act clearly—and also
know the action of God is equally clear—He will
do in and through you what He has done through
others before you. He is going to do that now!
Why again? You clearly saw how God works.
You clearly saw there has to be an inner act on
your part to initiate it. How? By letting your
Word be unqualified. By letting it be unconditioned by the world.

After all, Jesus stood in a world such as we
have now when everybody out there said, "You
can't do this. You can't do that. You can't have
this." And He said, "Oh, yes I can—by the
Word." I am certain that our friend Moses had
the same problem with his people. They all said,
"You can't have this. This can't work out. It
won't happen." He said, "Oh, yes it will—by the
Word." You begin to see how this thing goes?

To attain this absolute consciousness that I
speak of now, you have to have a kind of goal in
mind for yourself, don't you? I think this should
be your goal:

The Spirit of God, if allowed to know Itself and Itself alone through the Word spoken by Its executor—will always produce results in keeping with Its own nature. Yes, if that Spirit is allowed to know Itself alone through the Word spoken by Its executor, It has to produce results in keeping with Its own nature. You see, you are the *executor* of God's Spirit. When you *speak the Word*, have a sense of *releasing* this self-knowingness of God acting upon Its own substance idea. You are not telling God how. The self-knowingness of God, acting on Its own substance idea for the perfect handling of this problem, is coming upon you—is being fed into you. Get that *picture*!

Now, I am going to close with this point: We know that if we can be the channel for letting God *change the cause in a person's life, we can change the effect*. Think of this for a moment in your own surroundings with regard to illness, poverty, disposition, loneliness—that if you can learn to let God change the cause, you can change the effect.

When I was getting this material together I had an experience. It was a very simple one, and

I am going to tell it that way. At this point in accumulating the material for this chapter I happened to be in a park, seated on a bench, going over notes. Momentarily looking up from my work, I noticed a woman using a walker, a mechanical aid for learning to walk again, trying to get across the street without holding up traffic too long. I was on this park bench, and she was coming toward me from across the street. She was pitiful to watch. The more nervous she became, the more frustrated were her efforts to move her legs. Her nurse, though well-intentioned, served only to aggravate her problem.

I decided to see if I could help through speaking God's Word to her. Unbeknown to her, I decreed again and again as she made her tortured way past me toward the beach where she was headed—this statement: "The very Spirit of God within you by means of Its own self-knowingness, acting upon Its own substance idea, is now feeding that to your subconscious, changing the cause in your subconscious to one of perfect function for your legs." Think about that for a minute. "The very Spirit of God within you by means of Its own self-knowingness, acting upon Its own substance idea, is now changing the cause in your subconscious to one of perfect function for your legs." I was sitting on this bench, and I just said that over and over again. While continuing to do my lecture notes, I persistently came back to the Word I was decreeing for her.

An hour or so later, on her return from the beach, I was still on this bench in the park. And, I noticed that her nurse now was carrying the walker, and the lady in question was walking. Oh, she was not leaping up and down with gleeful youth, but she was walking by herself. And that meant something to me.

Now, you may say, "Well, many people do that on a beach. They allow the sun to invigorate their stiffness, and then they make an attempt to walk afterward." Maybe they do. But I like to believe that what I did as a channel had a great deal to do with the way she walked coming back.

I will emphasize it by saying this: A woman, following one of my lectures, was burdened with intense pain and told me about it. I recommended that she go to her doctor and be X-rayed.

I assured her, though, that we would be praying for her all the while. She did, and they found a tumor the size of an apple. Four days later they were ready to operate. They took X-rays, though, this second time—just before they were to operate. There were four doctors in attendance. Strangely enough, they could find no sign of the tumor. So my friend said to the doctors, "Well, you told me just four days ago that I had a tumor the size of an apple. And here we are four days later. What is this?" And the senior surgeon said, "All I know is there is nothing to be seen of a tumor now—not one iota." Now you think about that!

I trust this might wake up your power, the power of your Word. Start you on a career of beginning to speak the Word in keeping with the particular kind of description that I have given you here. Releasing this self-knowingness of God, acting upon His particular substance idea, in your case. And then feeding into your subconscious, into your "waters"—the real healing!

Try this out on your prosperity, as well as on your human relations. It has a way of causing things to happen that otherwise would not!

As I bring this *centerfold chapter* of the book to a close, I offer the following as your means of making it *indelibly* a *continuing part* of your life:

Your spiritual treatment either for self or another is basically self-contemplation of what God's *Holy Spirit*—acting upon Its own *substance idea* and putting it into *your subconscious*—is doing when you speak His Word.

Therefore, "*Only God*, by means of His *Holy Spirit* and acting upon His own *substance idea*, is now writing His patterns of perfect function ANEW for all parts of my body into *my subconscious*. And from this moment *only that* is happening to all parts of my body. And I will *act it out* both waking and sleeping. Nothing will *deter* me from *this exact realization* of my full healing. And the promise is, 'To him that hath [*this consciousness*]—it shall be given.'"

Therefore, "Only God, by means of His *Holy Spirit* and acting upon His own *substance idea*, is now *moving upon* all the *dark corners* of *my subconscious* dealing with *human relations*—and a million *shadows* are now dissolved as readily as one. In their stead, His *substance idea* is *in charge* of this side of my life and *recording 'in my inward parts' or subconscious* all that makes for order, harmony, forgiveness, and good will. From this moment, *only these new patterns will spark my actions and reactions*, and I will *feel* and *act* them out so that all others may know the *joy* that is within me. Nothing will *deter* me from this *exact realization* of my *new nature*. And the promise is, 'To him that hath [*this consciousness*]—it shall be given.'"

Therefore, "Only God, by means of His *Holy Spirit* and acting upon His own *substance idea*, is now *moving upon* all the *dark corners* of *my subconscious* dealing with my *prosperity and success*—and a million *shadows* are now dissolved as readily as one. In their stead, His *substance idea* is now *in charge* of this side of my life and *recording 'in my inward parts' or subconscious* all the *patterns* that make for *opulence*. This means that from this moment I will *feel* and *act out* this *substance idea* behind my finances, *stirring up prosperity and success* in all directions. Nothing will *deter* me from this *exact realization* of my *new opulence*. And the promise again is,

'To him that hath [*this consciousness*]—it shall be given.'"

In between treatments, should any aspect of your challenge try to take over your thinking again *with fear*, say to it, "Sorry, but I am doing business only with *God's substance idea* implanted in my subconscious, which is *in charge*!"

IX

OUT OF ALL YOU KNOW ABOUT GOD, COULD YOU BOIL IT DOWN TO THREE CORNERSTONES FOR YOUR LIFE?

Our subject is a most arresting one. We are going to consider "Your Eternal Cornerstones." I should like to preface the heart of the subject itself with a few interesting questions, so that you might get the most out of it.

Would you say that it is possible you have been sad recently? Been resentful? Been lonely? Then I suggest that you be converted. Not an outer conversion, a formal one—it rarely ever takes. But an inner conversion. Why? You are operating with a wrong kind of generator. Your sadness, your loneliness and your resentment are being generated from some thing or person or situation out here. I suggest you be converted—to a new generator. The One who knew it best said, " . . . that you may know the joy that is mine, that your joy may be made full." An interesting commentary on this is, that you are innately a happy person. That *inner happiness* draws happiness from the outside to you.

I used to know a person who was a kind of tonic to everyone. She had a lovely smile and was always beaming, at the office or walking down the street. And that can be dangerous. But no one took offense because she was just that way, and so everyone who came around her got a lift. I suppose we all know someone like that. The only sad thing about this person was that when she was alone she did not practice the same tonic on herself. She had the habit of describing herself as a "hot water baby"—as having nearly always been in trouble. She had a good generator going for herself—with others. But she did not have it with herself, so it was somewhat synthetic. You know, there are people who have a permanent wave for a smile. It is not really a smile. It is just a grimace, like that of a Cheshire cat.

Going to another side of your life, if you are in any kind of challenge physically, I suggest that with me you repair to a new generator. For whatever it may be that is not functioning properly is being generated from some belief which you picked up from the outer world. So I strongly suggest that you change generators. That you experience the art of being converted—not a formal religious conversion in the outer—but a deep inner sense of being converted to the generating of a Power that belongs to each and every one of us. Yes, "I am the Lord that healeth thee." "I will take sickness out of the midst of thee." "I will perfect that which concerneth thee."

We have a new letter on our desk since last Sunday. Another lady has witnessed the dissolution, the disintegration of a tumor in her body. Why? Because she has switched generators. That which has flooded over her is not a psychic healing. It is good in its place. You can remove causes through mental manipulation. But it takes so long, and takes so much out of you. What has happened, in and through her mentality, is not a mental activity born of the human. It is the spiritual action of God Himself—His Spirit at work. "I shall put my Spirit in you and you shall live." This has flooded and dominated her consciousness. Yes, "straightened the crooked path," the negative belief. She was not satisfied until in her flesh she saw the result of God.

Then too, if you, in business, find yourself at all frustrated, I strongly urge that you be converted. Again, not a formal conversion, but a real one, an inner one. Yes, switch to a new generator. For the old generator is putting in you feelings born out of people, situations, the times, your age or whatever. Which you have been dwelling on, and which in turn have been brewing this frustration. Convert to a new generator, which has the power "to teach you to profit and lead you in the way that you should go." Yes, which teaches you what to do, opens all doors and takes you through them. That generator, let it be emphasized, both teaches you and takes you! So have the sense that you have switched to this new kind of a generator. Therefore, there is now being generated in and through you a flood of power *beyond the human*. Yes, "Not by might nor by power [in the outer], but by My Spirit, saith the Lord," these things are done.

I should like you to try something here—which is an inner practice of mine.

Take your human relations, where you have been unhappy, and place them in a spiritual frame. Then look at the facts honestly, don't pretend, and have the sense of God changing that picture. Work up an intrigue, an enthusiasm— about how God will now change that picture. And He will!

Put your body also in a spiritual frame, face honestly what is wrong, and have the sense that through this new generator going on in you— God—the picture is being changed. Become intrigued and sensitive to the change that is now taking place—without any sense of telling Him how.

Finally, put your business in a spiritual frame, and honestly list there the facts of your frustration. Then have the sense once more of being intrigued, enthused and sensitive as to how God is now changing that picture. This will move things along with great leaps and bounds.

You may say to me, "This is all very lovely, but I need more details." So I am going to give them to you.

However, since I have been a bit serious, let me change the pace for a moment to one with a sense of humor. It is very helpful to relax and open yourself to your good. I think of a little boy whose mother belonged to one of the dominant religious sects. It does not matter which one. She was very desirous of her little fellow being converted, naturally to her particular religion. And he was! But it bothered the mother all the next day, for she wondered if his schoolmates that day would make fun of him. Get him to think he was some kind of a sissy. However, when he came home that night he was glowing. She said, "You mean to tell me that you had no trouble at all today with your schoolmates about having been converted?" And he replied, "Oh no, not one of them even suspected that I had been converted."

It is my fervent belief that when I finish depicting the generator to which you have geared your body, your human relations and your business—you will have no such experience as the little boy. Rather, those around you will know something has taken place. They may not know it to be due to this inner conversion but they will unmistakably see the change.

Now I come to the very heart of this subject. I am going to describe the generator in the most detailed terms and simplify all that you know about God to something that you can grasp and carry with you always—*Your Eternal Cornerstones!*

Everyone is aware, of course, that God is infinite. But the other things about God may not be so clear. We can all get a good relative realization of God right now. Not all of Him, though; that will take eternity. But we can get a good realization and a new start.

Well now, there are three cornerstones to God, no more, just three. These are not aspects of God. There are a number of those. These are cornerstones, and they can, in turn, become the personal cornerstones of your life. We have known about these three since childhood, but most people's realization is not clear. To do this we need to dwell upon them and think them through.

You and I do this with negative things already, so let no one pretend that he is not experienced in the art of dwelling as I started off explaining —any sadness, any resentment, any loneliness you are experiencing is due to the perversion of the art of dwelling. You are dwelling on things out here, and from that you get the results I named.

In the body, the perverted art of dwelling is rather obvious. A person is perfectly well; and because someone suggests at the office that he looks a bit pale or drawn, he begins to dwell on it. Begins looking for pains and aches he never had when he came to the office. Before the day is over, of course, he finds them.

By like token, dwelling upon things, situations and persons out here that seem to be the cause of your frustration in not moving ahead in business —is equally a perversion of the art of dwelling.

From here on, you are asked to dwell upon something from within to counteract the outer. It is fair to ask: Is it more difficult to meditate or dwell upon abstract spiritual cornerstones, which constitute your new generator? Is it more difficult to dwell upon these three new cornerstones for your life, simply because they are abstract— meaning invisible? No! Not at all! But most people assume such a holy pose when they get around to dwelling upon God, that they tense up. Now I want you just to relax and enjoy what is true of you—with the greatest of ease.

Omniscience, Omnipotence and Omnipresence are the three cornerstones of God. And they are quite willing to become the three cornerstones of your life. Let me interpret them in detail for you, from the Latin into English. They are the Omniscience, Omnipotence and Omnipresence of God. I shall now one by one, and in detail, lay out in the plainest of language the meaning of each.

You who have been taught to repair to your Deeper Self, or God individualized in you, for your healing, for the change in your human relations, for the change in your business—I want to spend as much time as is necessary to give you a detailed account of what it is to repair to that Deeper Self. What you should expect to reap. Why it is quite capable of generating a whole new you!

The first of these cornerstones of God is Omniscience. And that means God is all knowledge. Not HAS all knowledge, but IS all knowledge.

There is a difference between being all knowledge and having it. From Him all true knowledge comes. God, therefore, knows all about you. And all the things which, through Him, you are to know. And to know all—is to forgive all. God knows everything about the universe. There can be no new scientific discoveries that God does not know about right now. AND SOMETIMES PEOPLE WASTE TIME IN PRAYER TIPPING HIM OFF AS TO HOW TO DO IT. So God is all knowledge, or Omniscience. We need to think this cornerstone of God over now and again. That is how our soul grows.

I want you to be thinking it over now. You who are experiencing frustration in business. You who are held back by some person, situation or thing. Already you have put this in a spiritual frame. If you are going my way, you are going to be intrigued, going to have a wonderful enthusiasm as to how God is now going to change that picture. At no time will you tell God how to do it. Rather you will be intrigued as to how He is going to do it. That is why you have gone to Him. Because you did not know how. But as you repair to this Deeper Self, God individualized in you as all knowledge, you have repaired to One who does know how to do it. You understand this is happening to you. Let it!

Next, God is Omnipotence. That means that God *is* all power. Not just *has* all power. Thus in repairing to your Deeper Self, God individualized in you—you are repairing to One who can do anything without exception. Yes, God can do anything. That is more than our president can do, you know, and that is a joke; he would be the first to appreciate it. Napoleon and Hitler in their heyday were pygmies by comparison in power. You are repairing to all this power.

God does not have to prepare, arrange or rearrange in order to put something right in your body. Remember, here, the man who watched rheumatoid arthritis disappear from his hands and knees in a single session of prayer with others! So, no matter what the surgeon says, even though the diagnosis looks bad. You do not know quite what lies in the kidney, you see. Seems to be something awful. Yet God can fix it. Yes, God can fix it up *like that*! Make it as though it were not there. Just like the woman who watched her tumor disintegrate. That is, if you have faith enough. And you have the faith, if you will only use it!

When you pray, expect results from that prayer. Never postpone a date with your good! If you pray, and it does not all work out—all right, then pray again tomorrow. But do not plan it that way. Seek to get everything out of *this* session. Respond with your whole heart to Him to whom you have repaired deep within yourself. Feel your new generator flooding your mentality with the greatest possible power to get things done.

The third and last cornerstone of God is that He is Omnipresence, or, in plain language, God is everywhere equally present. To my mind this is the most important cornerstone of all. It means that God is not just on this plane. Not just on this continent. He exists throughout the whole universe. Perhaps one of the greatest instruments ever devised to study the universe is the present 200 inch telescope in southern California. What you can see through it staggers the mind. The big point about God being Omnipresence for you is this. There is no place in the whole scheme of the incredible universe where a person can find himself, where God is not! Yes, God is everywhere, and God answers prayer. Thus, there is no place you can find yourself, no matter what the situation, where God is not. Though you make your bed in hell temporarily—physically, business-wise or in human relations—God is there, saying, "Let Me be the new generator of your life. I can pull you out."

Now while God is functioning everywhere, Christ is not. Christ is the action of God in man. Christ is the Principle of God in man. We give that title to Jesus because he demonstrated it. But the term *Christ* or *Christos* or *Christolph* originally came from the Greek, the first translation of the original language of the Bible. And its meaning is *Messiah*. The Hebrews picked up this word *Messiah* for the intended "Blessed One of God." And this applies itself to you. Not just to the Wayshower, who went before you. Yes, it applies itself to you. The Bible tells us in effect, "In all places where you permit Me to record My Name or Nature, I will come in to Thee and bless Thee." In other words, if you allow Me to come into your lower bowels, where there has been a condition, I will come in and heal. If you allow Me to come into your business, I will come in and prosper it. If you will allow Me to come into your human relations, I will come in and harmonize.

Christ is not something different from God—but it can function only in the soul of a human being. Christ cannot operate through inanimate objects like rocks, trees, and so forth. These things are ideas of God. Beautiful ideas. But man is the individualization of God. That is quite another thing. It is why man has been given dominion over all lower forms. But though that dominion is indigenous to you, native to you, it is of no value until you let it become the generator of your being. This is your rare privilege. God does not act through inanimate objects. He may use them. But He *acts* through you. His purpose being to give His spiritual dominion through you to all lower forms of life—until "the lion and the lamb lie down together."

Think of it for a moment. You are the only creature on this plane who was created to work CONSCIOUSLY WITH GOD! Would you throw that all away and just work consciously with your frustrations, consciously with your sickness, consciously with your sorrow and unhappiness? Yes, you are the only creature on this plane who was created to work CONSCIOUSLY WITH GOD! Thrill to that—and begin to do it. Let Him be your only generator!

When the tree or the rock is used by God, it does not even know it. You see, an acorn does not even know it is a nut. The animal is also an idea of God, not an individualization. And before the animal lovers get on me, let me remind you I have two poodles, and no one loves his pets more. But animals are higher ideas, much higher than rocks, trees and so forth. You need only ask yourself if you would rather have a goldfish or a dog as a pet? You see there, quite clearly, the graduating degrees of intelligence. Now it is true that those of us who love our dogs often say, "Isn't he [or she] almost human?" Do not say that! They do not like it. They have seen too many humans.

Have you captured the magnitude of what I am talking about? Christ is not different from God. Christ is the individualization of His Presence, and It can only function in the soul of the human being. That brings It down to you, and makes you a unique focal point for God. You must never forget this. It means that you can focus the divine generator, which is deep within you, upon any side of your life where you need a breakthrough. Nothing can withstand the pressure of His Holy Spirit operating through you. Yes, you are the jumping-off place of God in the spot you occupy. If you have faith enough—and you have the faith if you will only use it—you can prove that God's Three Cornerstones can be your cornerstones to work out any problem in your life!

With these remarkable cornerstones as our background, let us proceed with authority. Be about our Father's business. And open our road to demonstration. The Bible gives us precise instruction. In Matthew chapter 21: verses 21 and 22, we read, "Verily I say unto you, ye shall not only do this which is done to the fig tree, but also ye shall say unto this mountain, Be thou removed, and be thou cast into the sea, and it shall be done." Therefore, we will not only put our new generator under all the sides of our lives that are not productive, like the "fig tree." But also we will let it generate full steam ahead on the *particular* working out we need at the moment.

What is the Principle involved here? It is something you can use anytime. I want you to feel that something can happen today—something good.

After all, God is good, and what belongs to God belongs to you. But we can experience this only as we participate. Your thoughts and your feelings are the creative factors of the Spirit of God ONLY when they, by your willingness, are participating with Spirit. Depression, illness, poverty and inharmony of any kind are foreign to Spirit! They are the results of something established in the subconscious by the individual. They are normal results from abnormal causes—induced by race consciousness.

In A.D. 400 theology, creed and dogma took over, and spiritual healing for all sides of our life went out of practice. In 1860 Phineas Quimby found something, and started the healing process again. What you should ask yourself here is, "Why should I be left out of it?" When you feel less than your spiritual "par," then you have to give perfect life material to your subconscious. What is that material? Why, the mood you carry to yourself! Your feelings are the reflections of your moods. You need to learn how to talk a *spiritual* mood to your subconscious.

Man, *without being hooked up to the real generator*—the Principle of God in man—the individualization of His Intelligence, Power and

Presence—the Christ—the Divine Self—*is just a man*. Because he, of his own volition, is limited to the human self.

Let us begin, then, by recognizing that the Infinite One is individualized in you, responding to that and declaring it to your subconscious, which is the jumping-off place in you of demonstration. Next, let us realize that what God does in the realm of His own Nature, He now does within you. Finally, because you are an agent of this Infinite Intelligence, Power and Presence, and are initiating this by decreeing it, you are one with God who operates by means of His Higher Law.

In you, then, await three things: your *recognition*, your *response* and your *declaration*.

Illness is the result of wrong thought patterns, which have become beliefs in the subconscious. Inharmony in human relations is the result of wrong thought patterns, which have become beliefs in the subconscious. Poverty is the result of wrong thought patterns, which have become beliefs in the subconscious. All this can be *psychologically diagnosed*. But finally, it has to be *spiritually cleared*. Where there is order and balance in the subconscious—health, harmony and prosperity must be obvious.

Here is your formula: You are equipped with all the tools to express life fully. That which you think and feel becomes law for you, and therefore an effect. Your consciousness thus is not only a law unto you, but it executes the feeling. This is realism. It is your consciousness, then, that makes you guilty of experiencing less than the Higher Law of God or His Plan for you. The cells in your body do not make themselves sick. The conditions in your human relations do not make themselves inharmonious. The situations in your financial affairs do not make themselves poverty-stricken. Yes, when your conscious and subconscious are in conflict with God—trouble appears. With a little cooperation in your conscious and subconscious, through the Word of God, you will come right.

Affirm for tomorrow a day of rich activity, and it will now come because you have let God be God! Do this tonight again, think of tomorrow as an experiment, and see what happens.

For your freedom from frustration in your

financial affairs, affirm, "There is a perfect action of God in my supply, my success and my business." Then, "I am one with the Higher Law of my prosperity, and that Higher Law opens its own doors for me."

If there is a malfunction in your body, affirm, "I am the stabilizing life-substance idea or know-how of God in action." Next, "The Infinite Spirit of God is living itself in my thought and feeling." Finally, "I now become perfect function in that part of my body."

In conclusion, whatever the problem, define *self* as the spiritual expression of life. Yes, I am a divine individualization, the divine focal point for God's expression. Therefore, what should I do? I want your expression, God, to be mine! Affirm, "I accept an adjustment of the problem in my life right now. That which is God individualized in me speaks Its Truth to my subconscious. I declare God is not in difficulty. Therefore I am not in difficulty." Then conclude with a sense of conviction. "Do I mean this? Yes!" Then relax, and let it happen. This is an unqualified statement. "I take my stand. I am healed! I am harmonized! I am prospered! A new chance is given me. A change of pattern in my subconscious has happened. I accept my good delivered unto me now!"

What have you been doing here? You have been giving perfect life material, harmonizing material and prospering material to your subconscious. You have been feeding the spiritual mood to your subconscious. You have been giving the feeling of wholeness, order and opulence to your subconscious. Now you have *not* been telling God what to do. Rather you have been letting God be God. And so it is!

X

THERE ARE THREE LEVELS OF HEALING, AND WE NEED TO KNOW THEM ALL. WHAT ARE THEY?

We are going to consider "The Three Levels of Healing." I want to discuss this in such a way that when I am through you will understand this field, and your relation to it as far as healing is concerned—so that you will have a wonderful perspective about the subject of healing itself.

Basically we start this material with the general question of healing; and that, of course, means setting things right in our minds. You and I should always try to demonstrate a healthy body, yes, as healthy a body as possible. Why? Because it is the nearest—or should I say, the first—embodiment of your consciousness. Without it, you do not do anything very well. You and I should therefore try to be more healthy each year. That is a valid part of being a Truth student. Instead of having the sense that you have used up most of your energy, that you are now riding on the little you have left; a Truth student should have the feeling of constant contact with the infinite energy of God—and settle for nothing less! In other words, a Truth student never settles down; he settles up.

The place to begin is here: We should give our best attention to the most urgent problem in our life. This is always nature's way of telling us where to go to work. If it is your body in general, then that. If you are out of a job, then it is a job you should be working on in your Truth. If your health is not bad and business is not bad, but you keep getting in rows with people (or perhaps I should say they deep getting in a row with you)—well, that is the something to put straight.

Some people in this field say, "First my body breaks down. Next it is business. Then it is people. Am I never to get anyplace?" Now if they mean, "Are we never going to get to the place where we do not have to pray?" the answer is "No!" And that is good, because prayer is a glorious thing. An interesting commentary on life here from a Truth point of view is this: Your business is only a part of your consciousness. Your human relations is only another part. But your body is the whole embodiment. It is involved with your business and your human relations. It is inter-related! So it is of first importance in your prayer work.

Now there are three ways to heal the body, and we need all of them. They are all good. And each way that I am about to name is higher than the one that precedes it. They are: *matter*, *mind* and *Spirit*. These are the three levels of healing!

Let us take the first, matter. Means physical healing. It is the lowest method. It includes such things as purging the body, massaging the body, the use of antibiotics, pills, surgery and so forth. This is the easiest way to get a healing. But it is the least lasting. To help your perspective here: Having been in this field a good many years, I personally have no quarrel whatever with the medical profession. I pray often for the unfold-ment of its fine doctors and surgeons. They are making rapid strides in their science. I trust that they, in turn, pray for those who are in our field. There should never be any quarrel, and I have none—because their attempts toward healing are from the outside in, and our work is from the in-side out. So the two should complement one another.

After all, doctors like to have ministers go to the hospital to visit. They feel it does something for their patients. Those of us in this particular field do not go there just to hold hands. We go there with the purpose of helping them have that resurgence of life forces from within. For we know that final and true healing is always from within.

Now the next step in healing is what you might call *mental healing*—sometimes called *psychic healing*. It means changing your thought, without necessarily having contact with God. Yes, changing your own thought, where it is needed. Mental or psychic healing involves your intellect. This changing of your mind, in your knowing and in your feeling, will work. But it is helpful to know in this kind of healing that there is more than one cause for the same illness.

Years ago there was a book called *Divine Remedies*. I do not know if it is still in print. It was a fine book, as far as it went. But this field of metaphysics is an evolving one. It is growing up, advancing, progressing. At the time, this book catalogued all illnesses in a certain way. It had a list of diseases on one side of the page, and on the other side the causes. For example, a nasty temper caused a certain kind of illness. Self-pity still another kind of illness, and so forth.

People used to love that book. They would get it out, read it—and find out what their neighbor was doing wrong! Now there was nothing really incorrect about that book of years ago, except that it went only *one-third* of the way. You see, there are two other ways to get the same illness, for which the book listed only one—disposition. The other two ways are suggestion and fear.

Let me illustrate how suggestion works. A little boy overhears the doctor in another room diagnosing his sister's throat. The doctor determines that she has a goiter. Now this has nothing to do with the little boy. But indirectly he hears about it. Later in life that preys upon his mind. You might say that he got an early start on the subject of goiters. It would not be unusual if he came down with this kind of challenge.

I use this example to point out that a suggestion given indirectly is usually much more effective than one given directly. Why? Because when it is given directly you put up a conscious defense.

But indirectly, somebody else having it as in the case mentioned, your defense is down and you listen. The world can sell you all kinds of things in this manner. So suggestion is a definite method of becoming ill. As a matter of fact, that is why some of our family heirlooms bear fruit. People have a way of saying, "In our family, there was Uncle Henry and Aunt Bessie, and they had this sort of thing. I never had it, but it is in the family, you know." Meaning, you are patiently waiting for it to show up. And so it can happen.

The third method by which you can become ill is fear. You may have a gorgeous disposition. You may not be laboring under any particular suggestion. But you have your own unique way. Somehow you have a general fear pattern. Much of it is known, and some of it is even unknown. With the unknown, you do not have the faintest notion why you have the fears.

Let me show you its effects. There was a woman who had this kind of consciousness. She was just a little bit afraid of everything—what was going to happen, and so forth. This was her life pattern. She had nine cats, and they all had St. Vitus' dance. Why? Because this was the tenor of her consciousness. That was the dominion she gave unto her cats. So, if you are interested in the mental approach to healing—be wise to disposition, suggestion and the general outlook of fear. These are three things to straighten out in your consciousness.

Also, in mental healing it is quite probable that the condition you may have could come back a number of times. But then it will go permanently, as you continue to establish a virtuous cycle as against your old vicious cycle. The vicious cycle goes like this: A person gets the appearance of his peculiar illness. Settles for the belief that it is his particular weakness. And simply lies down in it.

The virtuous cycle is something else: It requires that when you have the appearance of your peculiar illness, you admit it is basically caused by a belief in your subconscious—whether it stems from bad disposition, a negative suggestion you picked up, or a general outlook of fear. Having admitted the cause, you face it honestly. You declare, "I am not doing business with you any more. I am doing business only with a good disposition—or freedom from that old suggestion

—or a confident outlook on life instead of an outlook of fear."

Thus, we must say that psychic or mental healing is better than physical healing, even though
it takes a little more effort. Why? Because at least
it deals with changing causes, not just relieving
effects in your body, as in the case of physical
healing. To illustrate this: A person has an operation for removal of a small tumor in a particular part of his body. It proves benign. Relieved of
it through surgery, he has the timidity to ask the
doctor, "Will it ever come back?" The doctor
says, "Not that one—but you could produce your
own again." Get the point?

But in mental healing, at least, you are getting
at the cause. You are deciding then and there that
you will establish the virtuous cycle instead of
continuing the vicious cycle. All of which means
you seriously intend not to have the condition any
more—either inwardly or outwardly. So it is an
improvement over physical healing.

However in mental healing, since you are making this change only through self, you understandably cannot always do it immediately. It

would take a good bit of doing on your part. Rheumatism, for example—they have all kinds of names for it today. Years ago they used to simplify it and call it the "rheumatiz." But rheumatism today, whatever name they give it: suppose you are going to relieve yourself of this through mental healing. It would require that you change your thought from being prone to it—to thought that you are not prone to it whatsoever.

This is you talking to yourself. This is changing your thought about a belief that you have had for a long time. It requires being serious about your intention of getting rid of all fear of rheumatism. This would be your dedication. No one is involved except you. All right, now: that is mental healing.

Next, we come to the highest level of healing. Spiritual healing is the highest level, and with the highest level you always find the fewest people possessing it. Why? Because it requires the deepest technique. Many mistake mental healing or psychic healing for spiritual healing. Thus they call it *spiritual healing*—but it is not. In mental healing you never leave self. You never get off the ground. In spiritual healing, the work is done by God—not self.

Spiritual healing is the practice of the presence and power of God. When something goes wrong in the outer of your body, affirm that Presence and Power. That you are a spiritual being. That you are the individualization of that Presence and Power. Therefore, only God is in that spot—God only. If you were to get a strong enough realization of that Presence and Power in that spot, the condition would change immediately!

Why? Because the Grace of God, which very few people understand in religion—and which simply means the Higher Action of God, Himself—is released through such powerful realization. Yes, in spiritual healing, the work is done by God, not through mental manipulation on your part. And if you get sufficient realization of this, your condition will change immediately. Because the Action that is now released is above the time element of the mental plane. Is that clear? I should like to add that in most cases it has been my observation that the people involved get the full effect of such realization after their next sleep.

Now, I have given you as simply as possible the three levels of healing: Physical healing, the lowest plane, is good on its own level. It is the easiest to do. But the least lasting. Then, there is the mental level of healing—where you are the operator and you do the work. And finally there is the spiritual level—where the work being done is only by God. Here you see what the Father is doing and seek to realize it to the exclusion of all else!

I have tried to do this very simply, very plainly. So that I can now cite *strange healing reports*, probably current in your mind—and help you place them in their proper categories.

For example, the *psychic operations* that you may have heard about in the *Philippines*. That is a combination of the psychic influence of the doctor and the use of his hand physically. It is a combination of the mental and the physical—a psychic operation, yet with a physical action in it. The person is cut open seemingly by the hand of the surgeon, and the deteriorated inner part removed. This has been investigated and pronounced fraudulent. But still, who is to say how many were cured by this method?

Then you probably have read somewhat about *healing guides*. It usually is an Indian, living on another plane. A person on this plane makes contact with the Indian, and through him healing comes for all and sundry. That, too, is psychic healing—even if you go along with the idea that such things take place. Think it through. It is involved with your response to another person, who in turn amounts to someone who has passed over, seemingly, and who has a certain hold on healing action.

Now you need to think such a case through. Death is no diploma. It is just you going on. Death does not make you smarter. It is a sleep and a rest, in which you find yourself, eventually, with your head on the same pillow, going on. So, *you have what you had here—plus the cleansing of old "hang-ups," which the long sleep has done for you.* Thus it is possible that someone on the next plane has a certain hold on healing. But that would still be psychic, would it not? So you are short of God. It is still the psyche of the person to whom you are giving your faith.

Also, we have the *laying on of hands* to consider. It would be helpful to remind yourself here

that Jesus did this in the early part of his ministry. But not in the later part of his ministry. Does
that surprise you? I would think the reason might
be that people would come to believe it was the
hand that did the healing. Pretty soon, then, they
would have to have a blessed handkerchief sent
to them or some other memento for healing purposes. So that was finally left out. Just His consciousness of God's power so inspired the patient
that Jesus was able to say, "By your faith ye are
made whole."

But what conjured up the faith? That person's
faith in Jesus' ability to contact God! This is what
happens to people today in those vast auditoriums
filled with thousands and thousands. They get
caught up in an emotional thing. They have faith
in this particular person's contact with God, the
combined consciousness there, and so forth.

I suppose that everyone has heard of in-
dividuals today who feel that they have healing
in their hands. This may have come to them because someone in their family—a mother or a
grandmother—was gifted that way. And to all
appearances it does seem to be in the hands. *But
the hands are only sensitive instruments of the*

person's consciousness. It merely means that the person has cultivated the feeling that he is an instrument for God through his hands. Now most people who heal with their hands—no matter how they got started or however primitive may be their background—are emotionally linked with God. So you can say it is in the direction of spiritual healing, because there is usually this connection to God.

The person may have very little understanding of how he got this gift, but he has nurtured it. He has thought in terms of his hands as being such. He has practiced this. It adds up to fulfilling the axiom, "Act as though I were and thou shalt surely know I am." He has come to the place where his belief is such, and his consciousness is such, that he is an instrument for God on this plane. So that is an involvement of a person with his God. It may seem a primitive way. But if he believes in himself as such a channel, and that his hands represent the method he knows through which to release God power; he probably gets very good results. We just need to understand here that *the hands do not do the healing—it is the consciousness behind the hands, working with God.* "Putting hands on you" merely means this person's consciousness is laid on you—all of its response to God's power to heal.

The *strange case of Edgar Cayce* is something else again. It does not represent spiritual healing but rather a *unique form of psychic healing*. Should you accept the facts of his reported life story, as being so? Then by self-hypnosis he contacted the deeper layers of his subconscious. There he uncovered that he was an Egyptian priest in one life and a physician in another. From this vast knowledge he diagnosed cases and prescribed remedies that worked.

Now let us speak for a moment of *Phineas Quimby*, who is much revered in our study of Truth. It is interesting to note that he passed through distinct planes of healing by his own admission. The *first was that of mesmerizing*, as espoused by Mesmer: a hypnotic influence for healing—a form of psychic healing. *Then he graduated upward*, by his own admission, into another form of psychic healing or mental healing, *where he actually took on the sickness of a person and killed it within himself*. That is a rather hard way to live—hard on oneself. But these were his sincere experiences. *Finally he reached the spiritual plane of healing*, and as you know, on that great level he left quite a hallmark in our field—influencing many movements by proving that the healing aspects of religion should be taken "out of mothballs." Yes, somebody needed to rediscover it and reveal that God is just as willing to work through us to heal as He ever was. That was Quimby's great contribution!

Now I should like to ask you a good question. When healing takes place—let us say from the spiritual level—does it cut out the subconscious of the person? You see, the *cause* of the condition the person has lies in his subconscious. So you have let God go to work on this person. Does the work of God cut out the subconscious or bypass it? No! Spiritual healing does not break the law of nature.

Ordinarily, for example, iron does not float. But in ships, iron is so arranged with its higher law of use—that it can float. The same with rubber. Rubber does not float around in the air by itself. But when rubber is made into a balloon—it goes up. However, there an adjustment has been made to the law of its higher use. The same with the materials found in an airplane.

Now these modern examples illustrate something else. For the same was true with Jesus—when he healed the man blind from birth, the paralytic, the leper, the withered arm, and so forth. *Because of his understanding He got a powerful realization of this spiritual Higher Law of use for that part of the body.* That was all He saw. That was all He felt. Only to that did He give Himself. He made Himself an instrument of God—for this plane and to the case. Now, we all do this occasionally, but that does not mean that the subconscious is cut out or bypassed. By our powerful realization of the Higher Action of God, His Grace, we simply allow it to change the subconscious—as only the work of God can do, without a time element being involved. Yes, it will change it now, when we have sufficient realization of that Higher Action. "By Grace are ye saved through faith, and not of yourself; it is the gift of God."

Real prayer never acts directly on the body. This is something most people have yet to understand. They write in for prayers and they want their hand healed, or the throat healed, or the cells healed, or something else. Usually in a reply letter one cannot go into a long, detailed explanation. But actually the Higher Action of God, released by prayer, never works that way. It works first in the subconscious. It changes something in the subconscious—the cause of the challenge to the hand, or throat, or back, or cells. The first healing, therefore, is always in the subconscious—then on the body.

Some people say, "I don't care where it takes place, just so it gets here in my flesh." But it is nice to know somewhat of how it works. *Here you are giving yourself back to the original plan. God intended to work directly on our subconscious*, but through free will we lost ourselves to the world. *When you really open yourself in prayer, you give yourself back to God and let God pray through you and change your subconscious with His Higher Action*. Yes, change the cause!

Rheumatism, lung trouble, heart trouble—all of these represent negative vibrations in the subconscious, stemming from a parttern of belief that lies there. It may lie there dormant for a while, but it kicks up whenever the person goes through his peculiar trigger. Yes, then it becomes activated. You ask a person how he is, and that is often a mistake. He tells you right off. What he is telling you is, "I have this particular pattern. It plays its own music. And pretty soon, I am going to dance to it."

So rheumatism, lung trouble, heart trouble—they all represent negative vibrations from a peculiar pattern of belief in the subconscious of the person. Prayer, proper realization of God's Higher Action of healing, releases that Action into the subconscious—stills the vibration and changes the pattern. As the Bible puts it, "I will write my laws in their inward parts." Therefore, nothing is too far gone. This can still happen. By like token, the same is true of our home life, business or human relations.

It is good to remember, to put it very bluntly, that the body has no authority or power in itself for good or evil. It is a result, you see. Do not expect the body to get up and walk away by itself. It could not even raise its arm unless it had the mentality of the person behind it. All right, the same goes for your business—it is an expression of you. The business goes down or up because of you. The same for your human relations; they do not dance by themselves. You may say, "Well, I know a lot of people who dance to the wrong tune, and I don't cause it." True! That is their problem, not yours, unless you get involved through your reactions to them. Then you too are dancing!

When there is anything obviously wrong with the vibrations relative to your body or your business or your human relations, the greatest thing you can do is—touch them with the Truth. And if you really touched them through realization of that Truth, they would be gone forever. Yes, the negative pattern would be dissolved, and the vibrations stilled. *The Truth here lies in the powerful realization that the Grace or Higher Action of God can be both your Savior and your Redeemer at any moment of your life.* This is the Truth by which you can touch any negative pattern, dissolve it and still its vibrations. It will convert your subconscious mind there to the Higher Law of your being, the correct use, the correct pattern for your life. This is the reason for that wonderful old saying from the Bible, which I love so much, "By grace are ye saved through faith, and not of yourself; it is the gift of God."

So you and I want *to work for powerful realization of this Higher Action of God to do its work*. Yes, cut out the negative pattern of belief that has been holding us back in health, business or human relations—still that vibration, and write its own pattern or law there, with new vibration for our being!

Now I want to close with this: It should be our big goal to reach this powerful realization that lets God work! But in the interim, we live on *three levels—three levels of healing. And we must function wisely on all three.* It is not a bit of use to act as though they were not there—all three levels of healing. I have noticed that people in metaphysics who say they are above all other levels except the spiritual and have reached the place where they have no body—still have to take a chair when they sit down!

XI

DO YOU OWN A TRUE PICTURE OF LIFE
BY WHICH YOU APPROACH YOUR OWN?

I am looking forward to sharing this subject because I think that every real Truth student needs a kind of *monitor* for the outer world. All that is going on in it—the inane things that are being done—all of what you see that is so untoward. Yes, he or she needs a monitor. This is the special need of a real Truth student. And we are going to seek to find such in this subject, *"The True Picture of Life."* I trust it will become so real to you that you will ever hold it as your means of monitoring or evaluating life.

People usually look upon a gold mine as a source of power as well as a source of wealth. They look up to the term romantically, you know. The Bible does not speak of it in that way. But it does say, and it does promise, that we have a power within ourselves, which will produce the same as a gold mine. The Bible promises that through its means we do not have to be afraid, no matter what is going on in the outer. That we do not have to be sick, regardless of an epidemic.

That we do not have to be poor, regardless of the times. That we do not have to be a victim of outer circumstances, whatever the appearances.

Most interpreters of the Bible have missed the point. They say the Bible promises much, but after death—in heaven. However, heaven is here and now. In the words of the Bible, "The kingdom of heaven is within you." True, it does not end here. But it needs to begin here, if you are ever to find it. The Bible is describing heaven when it makes most clear that we have the power to freedom, to health, to an interesting and worthwhile life. The Bible promises all of this here and now. It needs to be known that its promises are statements of Higher Law of God's Plan for you.

Whenever you come upon a promise in the Bible, you should look for its polar or key words. Every such promise has a condition and a fruit. If you pass the condition, you must own the fruit. So, relate the whole promise to yourself by means of its key or polar words. That is a lesson in reading the Bible. I am just throwing it in free.

The layman is forever trying to grab, and then hold onto, happiness. Thus he loses it! Happiness is a result of continually unfolding. It is to be compared to a bubbling stream as the converse of a stagnant pool. Happiness has to be renewed every day of your life—much in the manner of spiritual power, which must also be created anew every day of your life. That is the secret of living with Truth!

I want us to realize this thoroughly, because there is a tendency to hold onto a demonstration in the past. Thus we make memory more than the continuing presence. When you and I realize that this power is individualized within us—that the contact to it is always there, *that is it a living, moving, expanding thing*—then we move right along with it.

So learn to think of it that way—as a living, moving, expanding thing. Demonstration will always take the form of overcoming something. You and I really grow by getting new demonstrations. We then learn to welcome challenges. To our challenges we should say, "Well, I'm glad you came up, because now I have the Truth by which to handle you."

Thus we learn to welcome challenges, because we know where our dominion over them lies.

The dominion of God, which is given to you by His power, does not mean that you dominate things out here. Dominion is the releasement of that which is just divinely natural to you— against that through which you are going. Yes, it is the releasement of *that which is divinely natural—what God wants done there*!

So you and I must learn to welcome challenges, because we know where our dominion over them lies. That it lies in the gold mine within us. Whether we call it the I Am. Whether we call it Jehovah-God. Whether we call it the Christ. Whether we call it the Deeper Self. Whether we call it the individualization of God's presence right with us. That is our gold mine. And we really grow by getting demonstrations from that power!

Those who are in this teaching—they are on the spiritual path. *Whether you are ten miles ahead or twenty miles behind others does not really matter. What does matter is that you are on the spiritual path. That you know the way upward and onward. That you are improving.* Thus showing forth unfoldment continually.

I believe this needs to be said to us every now and then as Truth students: We must be careful to put the loaves and fishes in second place, and the love of God and His purposes in and through us—always in first place. But you do waken your consciousness to God through each difficulty if you take it to God and His dominion within you. You see, the basic purpose of each difficulty in our lives is to make an adjustment all the way back to God. Only then have we really solved it. For we have come back completely to what God wants done there.

Herbert Spencer, the English philosopher, years ago put it very well when he said, in effect, "We try many schemes for finding the answers to life. They all have their places, and they possibly all help. But you have never really solved your problem until there is an adjustment all the way back to God." And so it is—psychology alone will not do it either. You have to get all the way back to God. Therefore, the key to unlocking the gold mine that lies within us is to know that *difficulties are only tests which unfold us Godward*—as we let them!

Here is a good way to look at these tests. As

soon as your difficulty disappears, you have learned the lesson. When grief disappears, for example, with regard to a loved one—one who has made his or her transition; when the grief finally disappears, you have grown through your loved one. Because then you really know the Truth, that you will see your loved one again if the link of love is still there, otherwise not.

Now the race, as a whole, is growing up. If you listen to television commercials, you may have your doubts. And yet the race is growing up. In the ancient world people were more emotional and less advanced intellectually. For instance, people in those days, who wanted to grow spiritually, entered schools. This was done in Greece. For example, there was the Pythagoras School. It had nothing to do with becoming a priest. It was expressly for unfoldment. Then in Egypt could be found schools for priests.

The teachings in the ancient world were largely on an emotional basis. The emphasis was on life after death. There was where you got all your rewards—with little relation to here and now. And the hereafter is a safe place to put such promises! The people in those days were not able to "bear it as yet," as the Bible puts it. They were unable to bear such simple reasoning as the following:

If heaven were on a cloud somewhere, and were so many miles long and so many miles wide—very few people could ever get into it, you see. Also, if it were a perfect realm, a place of perfection—that too would pose a considerable challenge, the challenge of individual perfection before entering.

Remember what they used to say peculiar to the religious sect you attended? "Well, we feel there is room for everyone, but the best places are reserved for the. . . . " Now if that were true, and you got into such a heaven simply because you belonged to a certain church—think where that would leave you.

You were still growing up. You were not perfect yet. You had a lot of nonsense still in you. You were a nice person, of course, but far from perfect. And you passed on. Now you get into a perfect realm. Somebody would have to get out. Otherwise you would mess up the whole lot, you see. So even a little bit of reasoning would throw that out the window.

Now, I have been humorous about this. But I often say, "I don't think God is so interested in what particular movement you grew up in, but how close you got to Him through your beloved movement." And that is the way to leave it.

This is a three-dimensional plane. The next is fourth-dimensional. But it is no more heaven than this plane. However, heaven can be found there, the same as here—*from within*. Yes, "The Kingdom of Heaven is within you," Jesus said. Life is a process of spiritual unfoldment. Each plane serves this purpose.

Also, in the ancient world people were taught quite a bit about psychic development. Every once in a while there is a rebirth of enthusiasm for that from the general public. We are passing through such a period now. There is nothing wrong with the psychic field, if studied scientifically. I have studied it at great length. Out of years of such research the caution I would share with you is this: Never get the notion, when you are studying psychic unfoldment, that you are studying spiritual unfoldment. They are two different things. People try to make a complete religion out of ESP (Extra Sensory Perception) for example.

Every once in a while, some forms of science get a new name for their particular field in order to get a rebirth of enthusiasm. And ESP is largely mental telepathy—reintroduced to the public. To read some of the books and hear some of the speakers on the subject of ESP, you would think they have traveled the last lap to God. But they have a long way to go. Intuition is about a million light-years ahead of current ESP. Intuition, properly understood, is not something that belongs only to women. That is a popular myth. It belongs to all human beings and is the greatest spiritual faculty you own.

Now I am not demeaning psychic unfoldment. It has its proper place. I have found it interesting, worthwhile and so forth. But if you are not careful, and unless it is studied under scientific auspices, nearly always the psychic will play tricks on you.

One of the marvelous things about the Bible is that it reveals the gradual involvement of God's Spirit in man and evolvement or manifestation of that Spirit. And that is the way to read the Bible—for the gradual spiritual unfoldment of man!

The point I am after now lies in this gradual involvement of God's Spirit in our consciousness and the gradual evolvement of it. It begins to become extremely practical in the Bible, but only when the prophets begin to do something with the Truth instead of just expressing its possibilities. Do not misunderstand here. Expressing the possibilities is helpful. Great inspiration for living has come through those who were our inspired prophets. And I have no desire to belittle them.

For example, *Isaiah* probably had the greatest inspiration of an accurate portrayal of what the "Truth that sets free" was all about—to be found in the *Old Testament*. But we do not read too much of what Isaiah was able to do with it. However, we certainly thank God for an Isaiah! Get the point?

Paul probably had the greatest intellectual hold on Truth through inspiration—in the *New Testament*. But he was a far cry from being a demonstrator of it. He went through hell over and over again—if you read his life carefully.

But notice that when we come to those who began to use and demonstrate the Truth—*Moses and Elijah and Elisha and then Jesus*—it was a pyramiding of such use. That is where the Bible really comes alive. Through these *Four Great Demonstrators*, one preceding the other and giving to those who followed the precedent of his demonstrations, we have the final meaning of what it is all about. Yes, there is only One Presence and One Power—and, through dwelling upon it as something individualized within self—*demonstration!*

Moses did that through "I Am That I Am." Elijah and Elisha did that through Jehovah-God. Jesus did that through Christ. All such names for Deity represented the *same premise*. These great souls gave to us the practice that counts: One Presence and One Power, and through dwelling upon it as individualized in self—spiritual dominion. Yes, that which is divinely natural (what God wants done there) makes its appearance to fulfill our particular need of the moment. This to me is where the great inspiration of the Bible should take us—"in earth as it is in heaven."

In Asia Minor, this is how foolish people could be in the olden days of the ancient world, in their religious practice: To pass the test of spirituality, those aspiring were asked to jump into chasms—blindfolded. Of course, the chasms were faked, but religious students still had to have the nerve or faith to do it. This was the whole point. The stunt was duplicated—using fire. Today these tests would be laughed off, except in fraternities and sororities. We find them there still. A throwback to this in religion is the snake-bite ceremony we read about occasionally in our newspapers—holding forth in some of the less intellectually unfolded sections of our land.

The old-time trade unions—not the modern ones, but those of former days—had some of these tests, which were more or less stunts. For example, you were asked to drink a can of paint—and it tasted like paint. But it was a form of tea, incapable of hurting you. However, you were required to drink it to pass the test.

Today, with our intellectual unfoldment, that sort of thing would be generally taboo, beneath our intellectual unfoldment. Through the demonstrations of Moses, Elijah, Elisha and Jesus, who gave themselves to the use of God's presence right with them and the dominion of what He wanted done—a great change took place in religion. The

great change amounted to this: The only tests
of spirituality were those that came by route of
natural events. Those were the only real tests
of spirituality made plain by the Four Great
Demonstrators.

The question that remains with us, then—
understanding that tests come through everyday
living—is whether you and I have sufficient unfoldment to meet the tests. These tests may take
the form of sickness, lack, unhappiness, frustration, loneliness or whatever. They are simply
natural tests for the purpose of growing up
spiritually.

So if you have one of these tests today, face it
honestly. You are to meet it as a kind of initiation
into higher unfoldment. Dwell upon God's individualized presence right with you—plus His
dominion. In other words, what God wants done
there. Gently insist upon it. Get your mind off
what is wrong and onto what God is doing there,
and you will become aligned with Him. In due
season your challenge will work out. Not only
will it work out, but what is even more important
—you will be left on higher ground in unfoldment. For example, I had the healing of my own

eyes, which many of my students know about.
Since those days I have, in gratitude, spent considerable time relaying the technique to others.
So it was more than a healing. I became higher
in consciousness.

Now let us once again see clearly how we pass
our tests, if we are to have the true picture of living. Our tests are what again? *Natural events
that come up through everyday living.* The important thing is: Are we able to meet the tests?
Yes, work with our God, so as to see that test
dissolved—and in its place, our dominion.

I am going to put the answer in the simplest
language. Stop thinking of the thing as
happenstance—that it "just happened" in your
life. And stop wasting your time saying to your
friends, "How could such a thing happen to a
nice person like me?" Yes, stop that nonsense.
Look upon it as a waste of time. Know it is not
going to meet your test. That all you will get out
of it is a shoulder to cry on—from a person who
does not have the way out either.

So you simply stop thinking about the thing as
happenstance. Face the fact that it is only a test,

which has come up for handling. Maybe you slowed down in consciousness a little bit. Maybe you let the world come in and tell you that you are too old or something like that. All right, stop thinking about it as happenstance, and face it!

What do you do when you stop thinking about it? You must have somewhere to go. And that somewhere is God. Start thinking in terms of His dominion that is in you—the divinely natural state to which you belong. Yes, off the problem and onto that dominion, off that which brought about your problem and onto that dominion which God wants done there in your life.

Above all, in your new thinking maintain an intimate relation with this Truth: that His action is now upon you—His action and only His action, regardless of the world. That this action is inevitably, inescapably and irrevocably bringing the form of fulfillment you need at this time in your life!

Then, when the test disappears, you know that you have met that particular one. And you know something else: That you have upped your status as far as God is concerned.

Error - Bad thinking as a human not Spirit!

Later on, more difficulties will appear. But they will be on a higher level, and you will handle them, too, and in an easier manner. Very much as in higher education, your first degree in college is the hardest. Your second degree is easier than the first. And your third easiest of all. Why? Because you have gained momentum in that direction. You have compounded that which counts.

When you get this CLEAR PICTURE OF LIFE, *you have the* TRUE PICTURE OF LIFE *for all time*. Once you have it, you know there are no more misfortunes. That misfortunes cannot come to you in the old sense. Because now you will look upon them for exactly what they are—not tragedies but stepping-stones into greater unfoldment in life.

It was not so possible for us to have this clear picture of life until Moses, Elijah, Elisha and Jesus came. They emphasized the importance of *use*—of letting God take over and express His dominion through us. In so doing, they did a work in the race mind. A wedge, so to speak—a way out for each individual that followed. Frankly, though, it has only been within the last two or three generations that a vague knowledge of Truth has begun to spread to the general public.

I am going to close with this: The Bible tells us that we have captured the essence of this teaching when we have the *single eye*—that is, when you no longer give power to sickness, poverty, outer conditions and people. In other words, you do not get lost in them, saying, "*They* did it." "The germ did it." "Circumstances did it." "I am weak and helpless before them." Yes, you do not give power to them. You know them for what they are. They are only tests. You have the power, the dominion. The single eye then also requires that you keep your eye of faith single to the gold mine within you, the individualization of God's presence within you—whatever name you give to that—and the dominion that is there. The contact to all this never dies. But you must use it!

All of which means that with this understanding, you intend to see the Word of God in your life, think upon the Word, feel the Word, speak the Word and be the Word—as much as a Moses, an Elijah, an Elisha or a Jesus. *Always remember*, that even if you never knew anything about it before, you have lived your whole life in terms of the word. The word—*either yours* or *the Word of God*—whatever becomes definite to you in your thinking. That is how all people live. *Whatever becomes definite to them in their thinking to the point that they do it or become it—that is their word*. But it is not God's Word—oh so much of the time! Rather, their word is established by people who have never known how to live.

But now you have it straight. The only means by which you are going to live life is—*by the definite Word of God*. I care only that you live by it—through seeing it (what God wants done there), thinking it, speaking it, feeling it, and acting it out. Just know always that it is the *Word's dominion*—its divinely natural working out—that is now going to fill itself in with every test. Why? Because the whole of God's Spirit stands behind His Word. And nothing can withstand the pressure of His Holy Spirit!

XII

SCIENCE MEANS THAT WHICH IS BOTH
DEMONSTRABLE AND REPEATABLE.
ARE YOU WILLING TO CONSIDER A
TECHNIQUE THAT CAN TURN YOUR
PRAYER WORK INTO SUCH A SCIENCE?

Those who do not understand the field of
metaphysics sometimes say, "The trouble with
you people is that you try to play God." No, that
is not the teaching. The teaching is that you seek
to *let God be God through you.* God has
difficulty getting through the person who insists
that he is only human. It is when you repair to
that Deeper Self of you for your help that the
outer self becomes a clear channel. Then the
things of God flow readily to you. But not to one
who just thinks of himself as human. Yes, it is
when you repair to that Deeper Self or Sonship
with God that you begin to take your rightful
place in The Scheme of Things.

*In your original creation, you were made in
such a way that God could move directly upon
your subconscious or feeling nature first, and*

then up to the canvas of your conscious mind. In this way, through His direct prompting, you were intended to live life abundantly and fulfill the reason why He gave you being. However, He also gave you free will. Thus you are not forced to go with God. You are allowed the leeway of growing up until you know that the only true freedom lies in doing the will of God.

So it is, then, that to some degree you and I have given ourselves to the outer world and its ways or will, and thus taken on its limitations. But whenever we repair to our Deeper Self of God, and of our own volition open ourselves to His substance or know-how or idea, we find our freedom and abundant living once again. I use the phrase, "know-how of God," because the word *substance* is strange to some people. Yes, substance is the "know-how of God" for human relations, for the body, for business. Its "way out" is above and beyond the human.

Each time you repair to that Deeper Self and open yourself, His know-how is added to your subconscious *as God originally intended to work through you.* Yes, you cannot spend a few moments of your time in spiritual treatment for your

challenge without the quality of your soul changing for the better. You have the highest teaching
there. Here you seek to become the Word of God
or idea or how He wants the situation worked
out. That is the highest teaching—because all of
the prophets, in keeping with the level of their
abilities in working out a case for another, sought
to be God's Word. Sought to be open to what
God wanted done for that person.

In your own mind, if you do not like the way
things are going, sometimes it is helpful just to
stop, be still, and say, "Is this what I belong to in
God here?" Yes, want what God wants done
there, and you have started His Word on its way
through you. Now that is practical!

Consider, here, something that you have
perhaps never heard before. There is a description of the Word which I love very much. It is
found in the Septuagint, which is the first translation, or Greek translation, of the Old Testament of your Bible. In our present Bible we have
an understandably watered-down translation.
Did you ever hear a story told? Then have somebody else tell it? Then finally have it come back
to the first person who told it? It is not quite the

same version, is it? That is what happens, to some degree, in translations.

So it is, then, that in the first translation, or the Greek translation, of the Old Testament you get a better description of the Word than we have in later translations. The Word, as described in the Septuagint is that office in God which takes what He has already prepared and puts it at the other end in man. Let me repeat that. *The Word is that office in God which takes what He has already prepared and puts it at the other end in man.*

Thus when you are in the midst of a problem, remember the promise, "Before they call I will answer, and while they are yet speaking I will hear." Yes, again: the Word is that office in God which takes what He has already prepared and begins to put it at the other end in you—for the healing of the body, the harmonizing of human relations, the prospering of affairs, and so forth.

An operation is about to be performed tomorrow, for example, which I am very conscious of at this time. I am letting the very beginning of it be with God. That He, above all, may be in charge. There is a wonderful biblical passage that I love for hospital cases. "Though ye make your bed in Sheol [or hell], lo I am there." Yes, if God is unable to reach you directly, and you need to use surgery or anything else in the outer, He will still reach you through such channels. In other words, "There is no place you can go where God is not."

So in the operation mentioned. I think of it this way: "From the very beginning, God is in charge. All doctors, nurses and aides are amenable to Him. God is working through all, through their brains and through their hands. Now the end shall be as the beginning—as God would have it come out!"

Now that is treatment. That is taking your Truth and using it. What I am after here is this: This Self of you, this Deeper Self, that you would become—its Word of God that you would have "made flesh"—think of it this way. You have a spiritual offensive to give to the world, which never hurts the world. You have a means, a substance, a way to release upon this world its very own fulfillment.

Yes, you own the ability, the mechanism for a spiritual offensive. You should not just be in the study of Truth, listening to it, and hearing it. You should have the feeling that you are able to *use* it. Yes, change this, improve that, and so on. Not by the outer self, but by the Deeper Self of God within you—His Word, His idea.

Now we are going to be very down-to-earth. If you and I were able to demonstrate over everything—we would not be here. We would be on another plane. But every real Truth student should be able to demonstrate over most things in life right here and now. Yet it is always amazing to me how many obviously sincere students do not demonstrate. They have been in this study a long time. They can glibly quote you *this*, glibly quote you *that*. But *nothing* happens.

Now the subtle secret is that they admire Truth, they love Truth, but they just never get around to *using it*. In that way they are much like an electrical motor—perfect motor—but someone has left the belt off. This point is a bit subtle because most people would say that is not true in their case. But if you listen to them, they give themselves away.

The fundamental thing is that you must first believe that God can do positively anything. Then you must believe in yourself as His channel. I say that because I remember a very good person, many years ago, for whom I worked. Since he was not getting better, I asked what his real feelings were about God. I found out what was wrong. He said that he believed that God could do anything, but he did not think that God would do it for *"the likes of him."*

That is all wrong. God is just as much interested in you as in the greatest person who ever lived—and potentially would do as much through you. Begin to believe in yourself. You are not as good, factually, as someone else until you have proved it. But *potentially* you are. And you must begin to act from that *potential*.

Once you get this straight—believe in God, that He can do positively anything—and believe in yourself as His channel—then you are ready to lay hold of this Truth. That God is on the job and at work in the particular spot where you need help, bringing about the demonstration in His own way. Or that only God, God only, is in the spot where the trouble was. Either method of realization is all right.

Years ago students of Truth used to get into a "tizzie" over the tense used in one's affirmation. Whether one was holding that God was bringing it about—or that it was already done. But God does not give a hoot about the tense. Some people do not either. God is interested only in the *feeling* you have when you make your affirmation. In other words, which is the more realistic to you: that He is bringing it about—or that it is already done?

One more thing before we really get under way. Remember: a book on the shelf, no matter how good—or a stack of notes in a drawer, however precious—will not demonstrate. Only that which you have *incorporated* into your *habitual thinking* will. Take it out of the book or out of the lesson and make it your *feeling* or *conviction*. Then you own it. You feel it only when it has become subconscious with you. Some of you may say that this is so obvious that you wonder why I even bother to mention it. Well, for the reason that some people "cannot see the tree for the forest."

Now we come to spiritual treatment itself. Treatment in this teaching is an exercise designed to overcome an illness, lack of a job, poverty, disorder in human relations and so forth—specific things with which you are hit. You need to know that it is an operation, and you must let that operation be going on through you. It is a much narrower word than prayer. While the word *prayer* is a beautiful thing, it is a *general* term. It covers the many ways by which you can be thinking about God or visiting with Him. For example, it could be singing about God. Or just being still and knowing *I am God*. Or it could be giving thanks to God while walking down the street. And so forth.

But treatment is designed for the working out of a *specific* case. It is a definite action. It is a definite operation. A definite, concrete, precise thing for getting rid of troubles. For overcoming difficulties. Or something of that order. Do not think that this is running after the "loaves and fishes" either. The quickest way to grow in the study of Truth is to use your Truth by tackling problems with it. Some people say they never bother with problems. They just pray to God and leave them with Him. The only trouble with that is—they do *not* demonstrate!

They are like people who say, "In our way of thinking we never celebrate Christmas or Easter or New Year's or Thanksgiving. Why? Because every day is Christmas, Easter, New Year's and Thanksgiving to us." Those are just words. Just saying something does not put you there. These official days are catalysts. They are there to give us a lift for the other days. So let official days have their place in our lives. And let problems also have their place. For they are there, too—only to unfold us.

Now to make this practical, I want you to take *the most urgent thing first* in your life. This is the way to give a treatment. That is, I am going to give the principles of treatment, whatever form it may take.

At this point, then, I just want to give the principles of treatment. Yes, the general principles you find in every treatment. Before you treat, you must select the most urgent thing in you life. Now you have a sense of using Truth. The first thing is: treatment must be definite with you. A definite thing, a definite operation from this moment. You are really working with God about that. You are working with a purpose. You are going with God to this new end: the overcoming.

Your purpose has a beginning and it has an ending. Beginning with God, it is going to end with God. Your treatment must never be vague, never dreamy. It must be pointed. You are working with God on that definite thing.

You know a surgical operation has a definite purpose. It better have! And so it is with treatment. You are going to treat your fear away. You are going to treat for your next true place of service. You are going to treat your heart. You are going to treat the gums of your mouth. You are going to treat the cellular life in the lower part of your body, where you have already had an operation, so that tumors dissolve and the cells come right in direction, form and movement. You are going with God there. You do not know how God is going to do this, but you do know why. Your part is being definite. Your part is cooperating. Your part is releasing His action.

I watched a tumor dissolve from a person in four days—going with God in this manner. A tumor with three doctors attending, and with pictures to prove its size to be almost that of an apple. Four days later these same doctors took X rays again of this person's body, and the tumor never showed up. The patient involved asked, "Where is the tumor? You showed me pictures of it four days ago." The senior doctor replied, "I cannot say. It simply is not there."

I saw that happen. Let it lend strength to whatever your purpose with God may be now. Once you start with this purpose, stay with God in each treatment until that end is reached. Do not go into treatment and then somewhere in the midst of it say, "Oh yes, I promised Mary I would phone. Better do it now."

The next principle of treatment is this: Put a gun to your head, figuratively speaking, and ask yourself, "Do I expect to get results from this treatment?" I do not mean that you are cocksure, that in this one treatment everything will be cleared up. But that you do expect to get results from this particular treatment you are now giving.

I have known people to do strange things in prayer. Some go through prayer like alphabet soup. It is routine with them. I always want to stop them and say, "Do you really expect results in this treatment?" You should! Remember that!

And if you do not expect results from any particular treatment that you give, do not give it. Wait until you are in a better frame of mind to work with God.

Another thing I want to say about treatment is this: Do not rehearse all the statements of Truth that you know. Some people's notion of treatment is just that! You do not have to go back to fundamentals in treatment. You go straight to the problem, and then you claim God's action—a direct affirmation of His action for that!

You know, when you took arithmetic in elementary school, you went through addition and subtraction and division, and so forth. Then, later on, when you had to use it for some little problem in the grocery store or something else, what did you do? You did not rehearse addition and subtraction and division all over again. You just used the portion that you needed for that occasion. And that is all you should do in treatment. Yes, use that portion of Truth you know for this kind of case.

Likewise, do not think all treatments are the same. Treatment for healing is one thing. Treatment for business is another. Treatment for justice is still another. Very few people know how to treat for spiritual justice, for example, because they are too much in the way. They use such an affirmation as, "Divine justice is now securing for me my own." But they are only out for themselves. Bother with the other fellow! However, they do not have any of God's action for justice until they understand *the way* God works for justice.

God works for the highest good of *all* in the situation—for the justice of all concerned. *Are you willing that the highest good for all concerned be done in the picture?* Are you really? If you are, *then strangely enough your highest good will come out of it*. Why? Because the action of God for justice will then include you. You simply do not have God action until you are *with God*. Until you understand what He wants, and are willing that it come out that way.

So whatever your problem is—the major one right now—use the portion of Truth that you need for this. Whatever your problem, go for the opposite of it. Yes, to the opposite statement in Truth. What you belong to there in God. You either form your own statement or you get a statement that fits your case. One that you particularly like. I happen to like the following affirmation for healing. I do not say it is better than others; I merely say it appeals to me: "The quick, swift, healing power of God's Holy Spirit is now mightily upon my _____, making it every whit whole."

Why do I like this particular statement? Because it has the three elements I count important. It speaks of *God*, the Source of my healing. It speaks of His *Holy Spirit*, the means by which He works through me. It speaks of the *spot* in my body, where I need help. And the overall tone of the affirmation emphasizes the *quickness* of God's healing power! Yes, "The quick, swift, healing power of God's Holy Spirit is now mightily upon my left shoulder—or my right heel—or my back, making it every whit whole."

However, if you really became one with God and said only this much: "This is healing now by His power." "This is prospering now by His power." *If you really believed it*, that simple phrase would boost the releasement of God's power to that thing. *Specialized wording* in an affirmation is *not* an absolute requirement. Only if specialized wording is *helpful* to your realization is it *important*.

How many times should you make your statement or affirmation? *The number of times is not the important thing.* For example, how many times does a mother have to call out for little Johnny to come home? She yells at him. She pleads with him. But he pays no attention whatever. However, when the mother hits a certain tone, Johnny comes running. Why? Then little Johnny knows she means business. She did not have to go through that rigmarole. She simply built it up needlessly. Treat your subconscious as though it were a seven- or eight-year-old child. Little ones like that are amenable to the gentle approach. Do it in an intelligent and almost cozy manner.

I once heard a lecturer who emphasized throughout his lecture that seven was the magic number—that you must make your affirmation seven times or nothing will happen. Again I assure you that the number of times has nothing to

do with it. You simply make your statement—
no set number of times—until that statement has
had an effect upon your subconscious. Until you
feel it there, *feel it to have risen to the Truth you
have declared.*

Then leave your treatment. Leave it for then,
and come back to it later. Also, *at the end of your
treatment, do not go back over it* or try to give it
a "once-over"—you know, an added thrust. Or,
you have been in treatment for a while—so many
minutes—and you say to yourself, "Perhaps I
should stay another minute." You are wasting
your time. God is gone. All this suggests you are
trying to take the play away from Him.

For most people *short treatments* are best. Am
I saying here that there are no people who can
pray long and still be effective? Of course not.
But for most people short treatments are best.
Why? When you are moved to treat, it is in the
beginning of the treatment that you usually feel
the most. And when you feel the wonderful realization that His action is there—then definite
work is done.

Your staying around and adding a "once-over

lightly" to your treatment is not going to do anything. Leave it. Come back to it later. And do not
plan for your next treatment. Get all you can out
of this one—as though you would never have to
give another one on that situation. If tomorrow
there is still more to do, then have another treatment. But do not plan for the next treatment. Go
all out on this one.

You know, years ago they used to say, "Use six
treatments." Why wait for the sixth one? Results
would be postponed until then, you see. When
you treat, remember this: *You will have as much
power in each treatment as you believe in God
and in His action in and through you!*

Now I am going to close quickly. I have given
you the principles of spiritual treatment for any
ordinary thing in your life. But once in a while
an emergency comes up—something big. Usually
with *big things* there are *three things* to handle.
Handle them with dispatch—*one at a time*.

The first one is *fear*. Go straight at it. Fear is
a bluffer and a phony. Remind yourself that God
is the only power. No thing, no person, no situation out here can do anything—only God.

Next treat yourself against any *sense of separation* from God—the sense of being a personality here on this plane, with God somewhere else. You are the individualization of His presence right where you are. And you have as much of His power through self as you will let God come into you to handle your situation.

And finally, you must treat the *bigness* completely out of your problem. This problem is only as big as you appraise it to be. No matter the size the world gives it. For you it has only the size *you* give it. And if you will let God appraise it through you—*then it has no size whatsoever*. Yes, no matter what the world says, it has no size from a cut finger to cancer—in God. With Him, there is nothing too big to handle, and nothing too little to be important.

When any negative thing from the world would overwhelm you with its bigness, there are only three things to handle. And do handle them. Handle them quickly. Knock out *fear*! Knock out any *sense of separation from God*! Knock out all *size* from your challenge! Remember: Your problem is only as big as you appraise it to be—

and you will get as much result as you appraise the power of God to overcome it!

Now that is spiritual treatment. Let it have a dominant place in your life. *Should any thought or feeling opposed to that for which you are treating* arise between treatments, brush it away quite casually. Like crumbs on a piece of paper. *Say to it, "Spiritual treatment works, and you are under spiritual treatment."*

XIII

IS TRUTH DIFFICULT?

You will be intrigued with the following material: The subject itself has to do with the question, "Is this Truth study difficult?" in this sense: Is getting results from it, or anything else about it, difficult?

It will be revealed to you that such is not the case. I am going to do the things you need to do with your Truth when you are working something out. I am going to do them myself—and in the tone and the way in which you should. Purposely, I am going to share this material with you very quietly and easily. For that is the way in which you should do it. Are you ready?

I trust that, in keeping with this material, you will make a test. Take something very important to you, that you would like to see made manifest. Now let me describe and build up the material that will handle it.

Perhaps the greatest irony in life is that man knows so much about the outer world and so very little about himself. That is true irony. But all the while there is a book—the Bible—that puts the following points better than any other book, as far as how to handle negative conditions in our lives when they appear—and how to live worthwhile lives. No other book matches it. Yet people, although they own the Bible and revere it, seldom read more than a few verses now and then. And when they do, they usually say, "Isn't it beautiful? Isn't it wonderful?" Then they unceremoniously turn the page with a sigh of relief and reach for another book like *Who Killed the Butler?*

Now the Bible does tell us how to live worthwhile lives by watching our own states of mind. Interesting? Yes, by watching what we are thinking about as we walk along the street, or find ourselves at the office, or wherever. Watching our states of mind. And the Bible makes it clear that this art of watching what we are thinking about is not difficult, although it will take a little bit of training, and that it is worth the price.

We who are Truth students must, I assume, already know this. But, even though we are Truth students, we make a mistake that is not too obvious. We seem to insist that the ability to demonstrate what we know through this study is tremendously difficult. Well, now, it is not so difficult as we have been making out—this Truth business of ours. Consider the following carefully:

The changing of our mind is not a question of playing cat-and-mouse with ourselves, but simply being Truth students enough *to stop*, whenever we find ourselves thinking negatively, *and change it*. Being Truth students enough *to condition* any negative situation that may appear in our lives with the "*Truth that sets free*." That simply means, think of what God wants there in the place of that negation. Ask yourself, "Is this that I have what I *want*? All right, what *do* I want? I want what God wants here—the constructive opposite." Then be Truth student enough *to condition* yourself to the UNCONDITIONED ACTION of God to bring about this spiritual working out.

I want you to keep *that phrase* in your mind as we move along. What we are after and what will cause results to come easily is this UNCONDITIONED ACTION of God. All it needs is to remain so through you. Thus your whole purpose is to condition your mind to it, so that it alone will be taking over. That is what makes the results come easily.

Next, I want to give you some illustrations of this:

Moses, for example, conditioned himself and the Israelites to this unconditioned action of God, when the need—to get across the Red Sea—appeared. Modern writers try to disparage that old story of crossing the Red Sea, saying that it was done through the subtle use of the tides. Well, that doesn't disprove the miracle, regardless. The miracle remains if only because the Egyptians, who were in a better position to know the tides, still perished, whereas the Israelites got across.

Again, Elijah conditioned himself as well as the soldiers of the king, all of whom at this point were dying of thirst from a long junket. Yes, they were dying of thirst in this particular land, and Elijah had to condition himself as well as the soldiers to an unconditioned action of God to procure water. Consider what he did:

To condition the soldiers, Elijah asked them to

dig ditches. Dig ditches to catch the rainfall that was going to happen. Now you just have to know that these poor soldiers—dirty and tired and thirsty unto death practically—when asked to dig ditches, had to be saying under their breath, "This man must know what he's doing or else he's surely going to get his!" So digging ditches under these circumstances, they were dealing with this expectancy: "No man could be stupid enough to ask us to do this—unless he knows something." And so Elijah did! A little cloud appeared in a cloudless sky, the rains came, and the ditches were filled to overflowing with the water. Unwittingly, the soldiers were conditioned to act out their faith with Elijah.

Now let us consider Elisha, who followed Elijah. Let us take an episode in his life. He conditioned himself as well as the widow who described to him this very trying situation: She was desperately in need of supply to keep her son from being sold into bondage for the debts she had incurred. (That is how they handled such matters in those days.) She appealed to Elisha, and he began conditioning himself as well as her. What did he do? He had her "borrow vessels— not a few." Yes, go out of her house and get all the vessels she could borrow, even though she only had a little bit of oil remaining in her house. Oil in those days amounted to means for bartering. As we well know, it is equally true today. And the necessary oil, in this instance, would save the whole situation.

You just have to know that as the widow ran around the neighborhood borrowing vessels, in her mind she was saying to herself, "Elisha is going to fill all of these. This is what must be going to happen." So the widow here is building up. She is being conditioned, you see. Then she was asked to pour out the wee bit of oil remaining in the one vessel she already had. As she did, the oil continued to flow until it filled all the borrowed vessels with sufficiency and to spare to get her and her son out of their difficulty.

Moving on, let us take Jesus for still another example of Principle at work. In this instance, He felt the need to condition Himself and the parents—as well as the boy born blind—to this unconditioned action of God. If they could get themselves clear enough, it would work. The parents were the stumbling block. They asked in effect, "Was it because we sinned or our boy sinned that he was born blind?" And Jesus said in effect, "Bother whether you sinned or the boy sinned! That is not important here. What is important is that the work of the Father be done. Yes, that we center our attention so much on His unconditioned action here that this miracle can occur." And we know what happened!

Now I would like to tell you a little story here that illustrates the point of all these conditionings:

This old Scotsman operated a small rowboat for transporting passengers across one of the little lakes of Scotland. On this day, one of the passengers noticed that the two oars of the rowboat were painted with the words *faith* and *works* respectively. Immediately the passenger enquired of him, "Why have you done that?" And the old Scotsman demonstrated his point. He did not say too much. He just took one oar and threw it away and said, "Now where are we?" You have to have the two—faith and works.

I think the Bible in its promise "With God all things are possible" illustrates this as clearly as anything in the Bible. It makes the same point:

That you and God are the two oars. That you have to work together. That you have to be conditioned to what God is doing—which requires your own proper WORK OF RESPONSE through prayer.

I think most people misread this particular passage. The Bible would not waste time saying, "With God all things are possible." Everyone knows that who believes in God. What we need to center our attention on are the first two words: *With God*. If you are really with God and have conditioned your consciousness to His unconditioned action—you are going to come out on top. You are going to have your demonstration quite easily. However, if you are going to remain "with your problem," well, take your chances, sweat it out. That is what it is saying.

All of which brings us to ourselves in a very down-to-earth manner. Most people allow the world to rule what happens to their lives. So it is safe to say tht most negative conditions which have come into our lives came because we let outer conditions condition our minds to them. That is how we have taken on all the sickness we have ever had. All the lack. All the frustration.

All the misery. All the unhappiness. Yes, we have allowed the world to unload its conditions on us.

I often say to people, "Yes, I listen to the news. In Truth you never put your head in the sand. You need to know what is going on." But I never say, when I finish with one station, "When can I get the news again? Which is the next station?" and so on—until 12:00 o'clock at night, listening to all the other stations saying exactly the same thing. I never do that. I want to hear it once to know what is going on, because I want to be a cause for help. But I never nurse or rehearse what is going on by hearing it over and over and holding it to myself. That is just taking on all this garbage, for that is what it is—the garbage of the world!

People who have taken on these conditions of the world to the point of becoming victims have not done so intentionally. No one does. Still, it needs to be said that these negative things are unconsciously taken on by us. However, they could never affect us negatively had we not let these outer conditions in the world so condition our own mentalities that we reproduced similar symptoms. This needs to be said, especially to Truth students.

Now the whole point here is this: Should you find such negative conditions in your life right now—would you just lie down in them? If there is lack, you need more clients, more supply, a job, door to open. If you are going through an illness, you need life forces stirred up within your physical constitution, more strength and vitality to be yours than ever before. If there are human-relations hangups bringing loneliness, frustration and misery, you need those "crooked places" within you made straight. Whatever the condition, I want to show you that results can be had there easily!

Yes, reverse your position with me. From this moment let your attention be on something that is going to happen—easily. This negation is going to go, and in its place a wonderful spiritual working out.

This is what you are going to do. Do not haul off on your negative condition or try to force the change for the better yourself. Just work easily and gently with God, knowing that what you belong to in Him is now coming to you! Now you have reversed your position. You have the sense you are beginning to exercise your spiritual dominion!

Understand that dominion. It does not mean dominate—that you are going to dominate the scene. That never is spiritual dominion. Spiritual dominion is simply releasing that which is divinely natural to you there. In any challenging situation, negation is not natural to you. And you are beginning to exercise your dominion. You are letting it come into form. You are not tugging or pulling or trying to make it. You are simply letting that which is divinely natural take over.

To put it another way. What are you doing right now? You are conditioning this situation, which you do not want, to the "Truth that sets free"—what you belong to in God there. What God wants to happen there in your life. You are reminding yourself that this good—to supplant this negation—already exists in God. "Before they call, I will answer; and while they are yet speaking, I will hear."

Gently and easily know, then, that it is already prepared. That it is now simply coming through you. As you have contacted that unconditioned action of God—let nothing in you stand in the way. Know that this spiritual working out comes through easily and well. So you are on the way out of your difficulty. Yes, even though what God has prepared has not appeared yet, you are on the way out of your difficulty.

Right here you have cleared the field of your mind from the old condition. It has already lost its sting. You know that old condition has no substance in it. Was not substantiated by God. You are dealing now only with substance, what belongs to you in God. What is substantiated by Him.

Now you have cleared the ground, so to speak, for a new arrangement in your world. Thus having cleared the ground, you are putting in the thing God wants in your life there. How again are you putting it in your life? You are conditioning your mind for the thing from God that you want to take place. You are inwardly conditioning your mind, then—to the inner world of God. You see very clearly the door to this good— opening and supplanting the negation. And the door to your good opens inward. You must realize that, because it opens inward, it has nothing to do with the world's limitations. So no more are you opening "Pandora's Box." You are opening the door that opens inward. Nobody can prevent that but you, and you will not! Thus you are truly working with God. And—"WITH GOD all things are possible."

Therefore, nothing in you is any longer holding back this spiritual working out, and certainly nothing in God. So think it through clearly. What your fulfillment is here. I do not mean to specify in detail. That would be trying to tell God how to do it. But have a KEEN, CLEAR THOUGHT of this good thing you want to come through. Really see it, and yourself in it.

Now, as you stand here at this end, letting it come through, also pour your feelings on that good thing—your enthusiasm, your great joy. This is working with your God. Yes, this good is coming. Love it in advance. Take delight in it. No effort. No strain. It is coming through. Feel that with your whole heart. I say love it in advance, because love has the ability to cast out all possible remaining fear in you that it might not come all the way through into manifestation.

Finally, act it out! Act as though this added good were definitely going to happen. If there is anything, after you leave this spiritual treatment, to do in the outer in that direction—by all means do it. Take those outer steps. Do them to the best of your present ability. But the important thing here, as you leave this treatment, is that you act as though this were really going to take place. No question about it. Yes, act privately within yourself as though this were going to happen to you. I say privately, because you need to keep it sacred between yourself and God.

Now what does all this amount to that you have been doing quietly here? You have been conditioning your mind to the condition from God that you want to come about. That is all. You have, in conditioning your mind to that good, been releasing the unconditioned action of God to bring it about. Now go about your business, and something will happen. Expect a sign to take place in this direction that otherwise would not—perhaps within twenty-four hours.

Why am I so sure? Because I feel you have truly conditioned your mind Godward, and therefore this unconditioned action of God that worked through Moses, Elijah, Elisha and Jesus is equally working through you. This same unconditioned action you have going for you now is what they had—nothing more. And in going for you, working in your behalf to get this thing done, remember, it does not deal in what has been wrong with your life, but only in what is right for your life. For example, it does not deal in the possible illness you may have had. It deals only in your complete wholeness. That wholeness is already stealing over you. First in your subconscious—where it is setting up the new patterns of perfect function for all parts of your body—and then, from there, into your flesh.

This unconditioned action also does not deal in any possible lack that you may have been experiencing in your life. This unconditioned action in your behalf deals only in supply—sufficient and to spare. And working in your behalf, it first begins writing the Higher Law of your supply in your "inward parts" or your subconscious mind. From there, it will work in the outer of your affairs, opening new and old doors. This is the only way it works, and this is what is happening to you.

Then too, this unconditioned action, now working in your behalf, does not deal in frustrating human relations. It deals totally now in your companionship, order, harmony, freedom and great joy. I want you to feel that with me. First, this unconditioned action is building up in you these states of consciousness in your subconscious —companionship, order, freedom and great joy. And now it is opening up in your outer world that which is comparable to what is in your new, inner world. Nothing can stop this but you, and you are staying true! In other words, this unconditioned action now released in your behalf does not deal in how difficult human relations in your life may have been, but only in the "life more abundant." That portion of its great human relations you may need at this time.

After all, the aforementioned prophets— Moses, Elijah, Elisha and Jesus—stood THEN even as you stand NOW: in the midst of a conditioned world. A conditioned world which said, "That for which you pray can't happen. It's impossible." But the prophets replied in effect, "Yes it can—by an unconditioned action of God through me that can and will do it—and nobody can stop it but me, and I continue to say yes to God."

And so it was that the Red Sea parted or the tide went out—whichever you prefer—but the miracle happened in either case. At another time, a little cloud appeared where before there was only a cloudless sky. Then the rain fell, and in so doing filled the ditches so that soldiers dying of thirst were saved. On another occasion, we remember, the borrowed vessels did not remain empty. The oil continued to pour until there was sufficiency and to spare. Also, there was the incident of the Scribes, who scoffed at what was about to happen to a blind man's eyes. This is what took place: The man himself remained open to the unconditioned action of God and said in effect, "All I know is that once I was blind and now I see."

And so will you, peculiar to your current need, experience the result that you are after— EASILY. Yes, "Behold I will do a new thing through you: now it shall spring forth; shall ye not know it?"—and you do! So a sign in the direction of that spiritual working out will appear. Perhaps within the next twenty-four hours. Look for it!

XIV

The purpose of this book has been to clarify
even further all that we have going for us to handle what is a horrendous task for many people—
but which can be made pleasurable! What is that
task? All problems come under one of three headings: people, situations and things. Not four, just
three. And usually people are the most difficult.
Not that people really are. We simply let them
be!

Now, if you want a joyous, happy, harmoni-
ous, healthy, prosperous and successful life—you
must handle these *three things*. Got to learn to
handle *people*. Got to learn to handle *situations*.
Got to learn to handle *things*.

Let me go over this for a little bit: Instead of
reacting automatically to these three, we must
learn how to react properly. That is the secret of
being a Truth student. For example, if up to now
your reaction is anger—when there are things to

make you angry—remember you are simply dealing with a race reflex action. That is what the
race would do. It requires no brains whatsoever.
This will help you. Going down the line, if your
reaction by like token is annoyance—the same:
Requires no brains. If something becomes dangerous, and you get fearful—again, you win no
prize. That is what most everyone else would do.
That is what the race would do. If things get
difficult, and you get discouraged, that too, is
simply a reflex. It requires no ability whatsoever.
All this simple race reflex thinking must go out of
the system of a Truth student. And he or she must
learn *to react by choice thinking*. Choice thinking would be not being angry—but knowing how
to achieve this. Not being annoyed, not being
afraid, not being discouraged—for here the
Truth student is using *his God-given dominion*.
And dominion is not dominating anything. It is
simply releasing that which is divinely natural.
Always remember that. This is your God-given
dominion, *used*.

Now I want you to boil that down in your
mind. *Dominion lies in just what thoughts and
feelings you will entertain when challenges arise.*
Of course, this is a little difficult at first. No one

starts out able to do this. But any one of you can do it! You can train yourself to throw out these negative race reflexes. Just remember, they require no brains whatever. It is quite possible that a tendency toward them will come back several times. So what! They will go shortly if you mean business, and you will come back into the most priceless of all things—your dominion.

To get this dominion, the *first requisite* is to want it. Automatically you may say, "Of course I want it." But the point is, do you? Do you really want this dominion? If you don't, God won't force it on you. You can go right along with the race. But, if you do want this dominion, you are going to have greater happiness than you have ever known. For there will be no time out for those wasted emotions. If you don't want this dominion, hear me out: You are going to have the same old troubles. But, if you do want it— greater happiness than you have ever known.

Now let me go over that for a moment. There is a very helpful way to correct yourself, *if you don't want this dominion yet*—a very honest way. And I think you might like it. Listen to this carefully: If you don't really want it yet, if you are going to go right on saying, "Everybody else does this, so why not me?" just be very honest with yourself, and say, "I could have poise here instead of anger, *but I don't want it yet*. I like to tell people off." That is being fair. Or this: "I could have tranquility, *but I don't want it yet*. I like being disturbed by every little thing that comes up. That's a real specialty of mine." Be honest about it, you see. Or, "I could have a divine sense of protection, you know, every time I go out on the street or out at night. I could have it, *but I don't want it yet*. I like things out here to make me afraid." And here is a very good one: "I could have the permanent conviction of a winner." *How about that?* "I could have the permanent conviction of a winner, whatever I do. *But I don't want it yet*. I like being discouraged every time things get a little bit difficult. Other people are like that. Why not me?" This is very good therapy, and it is honest. All right. That is the business of wanting it, this dominion!

The *second requisite* for getting this dominion is to go all out for it. How do you do that? Well, just start right out for it! Yes, make up your mind once and for all that you want choice thinking instead of race reflex thinking. First of all, you are not going to let anything make you angry. Not going to talk about it; just going to set it up in your mind. A wonderful thing now will begin to take place for you. The very fact that you are not angry gives you the chance for victory, whatever the situation—the victory of releasing the power, the action of God there through you. For God works best through the person who is at *peace* when he would otherwise be angry.

Here is an added tidbit on this business of going all out for your dominion; it is a standard Truth statement that will stand the test of time: "When you do not react emotionally to a challenge, you can always win out." Trust you may always remember that. Yes, when you do not react emotionally to a challenge, you see—rather, think before you speak or think before you act or react—you can always win out. And this refers to any of the emotions—anger, fear, jealousy, hopelessness, even hate. For you see, all of these negative virtues that we indulge in from the race simply disarm us. They make us liable to the worst. Always have. Another little helpful point here about yourself that will help others is that when you react by choice thinking instead of just your emotions, it helps the other fellow too, who may otherwise be quite willing to give you a hard time. How does it help him? Well, when you stop to think before you speak, act or react, if you are wrong, you will come to see it where otherwise you would not. And if you are not wrong, you will be shown how to help the other fellow correct himself. You will be shown something to do. Sounds challenging, but it really works.

To illustrate, an old friend of mine used to be a football great. Was a most powerful man. Driving one day in the rain he almost collided with another man driving under the same handicap. What was my friend's reaction? He was all for climbing out of his car and thrashing him. But the other fellow *merely smiled* and *wiggled his finger through his window glass.* On arriving home that night, my friend told his wife, "You know, today I met a better man."

Be open here, because it will give you an incentive to try out this dominion and give you a clear picture of what it is going to do for you if you can really see it. So now just this little helpmate, please. You may say this is going to be dull. Oh, no. This is the path to freedom, to progress, to harmony, to mastery of self, and to real peace of mind. Is that not worth having? When you achieve this, when you find yourself doing it, you are at that moment literally—not potentially—what the old-time poet called, "the Captain of your soul." Here you really are in charge! And it's a great feeling!

There are many other advantages to this killing out of these old negative reflexes. For one thing, it automatically opens you to the positive of life as never before. It puts you on the new side of the ledger. Another thing: when you begin to get rid of these old reflexes that you picked up along the way, you now know them for what they are—*sheer junk*. Then, too, many joys you have never known will begin to come to you, joys that have been out of your life. They now have to happen.

So regardless of whether your problem is a person, situation or a thing, here is the program you are after: react by choice, not race reflex thinking any more. This is truly going to work to handle the problems of life as a member of a higher breed. Now, just to make this worthwhile

—this little program that I have set for you—let us just take a brief look at the opposite. Look back for just a moment—but for good therapy.

The opposite of doing what I have brought to your attention would be to say about your employment, for example, "I hate my job because it bores me. Hate my employer. He should treat me better, so I do as little as I can. That's the way I feel about it." All right. "Also, I waste a little material here and there, just to get even." Now, where are you? On the way to getting fired. It may take a while, because no matter how good you are or brilliant, your attitude is very, very important. Don't ever forget that. Some of the most brilliant people I have known *never made it* because they had the *wrong attitude*. If you are with some company, you better have the attitude of being for it while you are there. This business of getting back at your employer is a waste of time. It is plain junk. Certainly such an attitude, if it doesn't lose you your job, isn't going to prepare you for a better one. You are practicing the wrong thing.

The main thing to remember, before we leave this point, is that the whole idea in any of these headings, whether it be *people*, *situations* or *things*, is that you do not let yourself any more become angry, annoyed, afraid and discouraged. These may slip up on you, but keep remembering that they are a waste. And I would have to be the first to admit to you that the lower self of you, who may have been dormant for awhile—could still want to be the way it is. You know the old saying, "I don't care about anything, I am what I am." But while you are saying that, the I AM that Moses knew, that Jesus knew, that all the greats came to know—I AM THAT I AM, the real I AM that could make you a captain—*does not want to be that way*! "Me" may want to be-cause he is still just growing up; but "I AM," which you really are, does not! Here you are dealing with a Self that is cut from a higher mold. And in our hearts we all aspire to be this—be the best.

Now here is a little technique that will help you when the old in you says, "I'm going to go my old way even though I know better": *You don't do battle* when that crisis appears; *you just choose*. That is all. After all, you cannot wrestle with error without getting contaminated—any more than a chimneysweep can do his job without getting soot on himself. So don't do battle, just choose. Certainly God does not do battle with your challenge in healing you. And if you want to go with God, don't battle with your lower self—just choose. Then you are letting God take over.

There are many ways of talking about these old negative race reflexes, and I think it is good because they represent wrong outlooks that we can stumble into and get caught up in without knowing it. If you worry—that is a reflex. Some people say, "I have to worry to get something done." No you don't. You are doing it the hard way. That is the time really to pray and open yourself to God. You have a brain, but you are not the Mind. God is the Mind. You want to let that Mind flow into your brain—to give you the idea for the way out!

A young fellow was going to college at the time when I taught in this direction in Boston. His dad asked him, "What do you get out of that fellow?" He said, "Well, in that particular lecture he gave, one thing stuck with me. It is this: Instead of you worrying about it, let God worry about it. He knows how to handle it. If I let Him, then my brain is going to get the idea of what to do. It is not going to get that if I just keep going over the stuff and nonsense I am going through."

I think one of the greatest single lines that I know—for not battling, just choosing—is this: The time that you stop to think is a kind of moment of prayer. Here you are not going to be the old you, you are going to try to be what God would want you to be. It is being that higher breed. So here is this idea again: The moment that you stop to think—instead of just going head on into the anger or annoyance or whatever— you are in prayer. It may not seem to you that you are, but in being still for a moment before you think, speak, act or react, you are open to God instead of just going the way of the race. And this is what I want you to remember: From that very second, God is doing His wonderful thing through you. He is at work. The heat is on the problem, and no longer on you. It is like putting tomato soup on the hot stove for cooking. Once you have put it there, let it sizzle. Don't try to make it happen yourself. By like token, once you have gone to God, let yourself sizzle from

God. You will find more and more that you don't have to make yourself do the right thing. You will just do it!

I think it is well explained this way: When you take that moment to be still, God begins to pray through you, whether you use that term or not. Yes, God begins to move through you, and you start revising your attitude. What you otherwise would have done, you don't do—whether it is a person, situation or thing—because God is now moving through your thought. It is no longer race reflex thinking with you. In that moment you will revise what you would think or do, and you will know that in this way it will be handled. Always remember that when you go with God in that manner, you are going the way out of trouble. Never mind how God is going to do it. That is God's business. Your business is simply to choose His way out. Then all power in heaven and earth will begin to be given you, and all things will be put right from His leadings.

So let us conclude with this:
(1) With God there is always a way out.
(2) Divine wisdom can and will do it.

(3) There is nothing that prayer cannot overcome.

(4) There is no delay in God.

(5) There is nothing too late for Him to handle.

A good illustration here would be that of a child learning arithmetic—learning to take 4 from 6, and 6 from 8. Then he finally attempts 8 from 10. Gets lost trying to do that. Says, "Impossible." But the teacher knows a *dodge* the child does not. She simply explains the *numeral 10* to him.

Well, we are like that. God has a *dodge* we do not know as yet—a way we have yet to conceive.

You know, too many people go through life slumbering. They react automatically to every situation. Just what is usually done—that is all they ever do. They are asleep for all practical purposes. Above all, they are asleep to God. They are like the story of the Lord Chancellor of England, who dreamed that he was addressing the House of Lords. And when he awoke, he was!